Praise for *Mix*

"The book is true to its mission of delving into the heart of multicultural, multiethnic couples. The authors skillfully blend psycho-education and real life couple stories that go beyond just teaching, more like opening the heart."

> – Terry Pfannenstiel, Ph.D., Senior Clinician, Pawnee Mental Health Services; Adjunct Professor, Kansas State University

---

"I am a film maker who has traveled the world and lived abroad. My life has been filled with relationships with people of many cultures. My current film, *Look At Us Now, Mother!*, reaches deeply into my own ethnic culture and the challenges that I have faced. Harriet and Rhoda's work on this topic is not only cutting edge but so needed to help our growing population of multiethnic individuals and relationships. With their combined years of work and wisdom, we are lucky to have their knowledge passed on to us."

> – Gayle Kirschenbaum, multiple award-winning writer, producer, and director of documentary films, including *My Nose* and *A Dog's Life: A Dogamentary* www.kirschenbaumproductions.com New York, New York

"I related to lots of things whilst reading *Mixed Blessings*. For example, I recognized I've gone through the acculturation process working in Iraq and Afghanistan. I also realized that I still do a lot of cultural refueling even after living in Thailand for several years."

— David S., a Scotsman living
in Southeast Asia

"*Mixed Blessings* addresses the intense feelings of being 'neither/nor' when individuals are forced to respond to the difficult question of what is considered home or 'homeland.' The book illustrates how couples can negotiate and reconcile the conflict between being loyal to their individual selfhoods versus the expectations of their extended families."

— Cristina Fandino Ed.D., an Argentine Canadian
psychologist

Mixed BLESSINGS

A Guide to Multicultural and Multiethnic Relationships

Rhoda Berlin, MS, LMFT
Harriet Cannon, M.C., LMFT, LMHC

Published by Mixed Blessings, LLC, Seattle, Washington, USA

PUBLISHER'S NOTE
All examples and stories in *Mixed Blessings* are fictional. Any resemblance to actual persons, living or dead, events, or locales is entirely coincidental.

ISBN: 0989522903
ISBN-13: 9780989522908

Library of Congress Control Number: 2013911840
Seattle, WA, USA

Cover design and interior graphics by Ned Cannon
Back cover photograph by Barry Scharf

Published in the United States by
Mixed Blessings, LLC
Seattle, Washington, United States of America
www.mixed-blessings.com

For our families, with love.

All you need is love
There's nothing you can do that can't be done
Nothing you can sing that can't be sung
It's easy
Love is all you need

– John Lennon/Paul McCartney

You like potato, and I like po-tah-to,
You like tomato and I like to-mah-to—
Potato, po-tah-to, tomato, to-mah-to!
Let's call the whole thing off!

– Ira Gershwin

CONTENTS

ACKNOWLEDGMENTS

We were born into families who lived mixed blessings in their relationships, traveled, migrated, and influenced us to examine who we are and why we hold the beliefs we do. Therefore we start with heartfelt thanks to our parents, Frank, Mary, Grace, and Mulka.

To our husbands, Hermann Berlin and Charlie Cannon, for their faith in us and their patience with the three-year evolution from idea to publication of *Mixed Blessings*. To Charlie Cannon for his drafting expertise on our developmental table and Culturegram figures.

To our readers, Jenny Berlin, Jessica Berlin, Julie Berlin, Maurice Pigaht, Barbara Johnstone, and Mary Merralls, for their invaluable feedback and encouragement.

To our editor, Sarah Kishpaugh, who edited multiple drafts and honed and helped us clarify our language and our message into something we are proud to present.

To our graphics designer, Ned Cannon, for his creative spirit and humor working with a couple of psychotherapists.

To our family and friends, too numerous to mention here, who always believed in us and supported us when we were overwhelmed by the enormity of what it takes to complete and publish a book.

Last but not least, a profound thank you to our clients of the last twenty-five-plus years, who have taught us much and for whom we have the deepest respect.

INTRODUCTION

It's natural to judge by appearances. Humankind's tendency to quickly determine whether someone is white, black, Asian, or Latino has pervaded daily living, seeping into the media, education, and entertainment industries. Nonetheless, as therapists we know people want to be understood and accepted for the many cultures, ethnicities, and regional experiences that make up the whole of their person. In today's multicultural landscape, first impressions no longer suffice.

Our mission in *Mixed Blessings* is to delve into the heart of what it means to be a multicultural, multiethnic couple. We will look at educational self-help aspects of themes we have encountered in our collective fifty-plus years as counselors, and we will highlight these relationship issues using examples based on real life.

We are neither academics nor formal researchers, yet between the two of us we have lived and traveled across the globe and resided in several regions of the United States. We are conversational in multiple languages. We know what it means to live and work across cultures and ethnicities and to have the wherewithal it takes to thrive. Included are our own personal stories, which describe our separate paths and the drive that led us to write this book.

The structure of *Mixed Blessings* includes two parts and a resource section. Part 1 is what we in the counseling field call "psychoeducation."

That means we will look at the big picture of couple issues using developmental, sociocultural, and anthropological concepts. This is complex stuff. It might tangle your brain in knots. You may want to read it again after reading part 2, to put it all together in a way that works for you. In the end, we hope the psychoeducational information can be a validation, a welcome relief, a life raft, or a reference on your relationship journey.

Part 2 is a collection of twelve stories told in the voices of twelve fictionalized couples from a variety of cultural backgrounds, ethnicities, and educational and life experiences. All of the stories are inspired by actual relationship challenges couples have brought to our offices. In each of the couples' stories we have added counselors' perspectives that proved helpful and thoughts on ways to apply them in your own relationship.

Part 3 of *Mixed Blessings* is a nonexhaustive resource section. There is so much out there to discover in libraries and on the Internet that we can't begin to include it all. These resources are a few of our favorites, and we have used them successfully over the years. We hope you find them helpful.

We have a broad philosophical interpretation of multicultural and multiethnic relationships and hope you enjoy the journey through *Mixed Blessings* as we introduce real life situations through the voices of fictionalized couples from diverse backgrounds. To give you a taste of what is to come, we introduce you to nine couples living *Mixed Blessings*. Each couple offers different perspectives on what it is to be a multicultural or multiethnic couple. Their diversity is precisely what we celebrate and explore throughout the book.

Keeping the Faith: Karen and Glen

Karen and Glen married in their early fifties, much to the chagrin of their grown children. The wedding was small, a celebration with friends with a potluck at home in Little Rock, Arkansas. Before their second anniversary, Glen's employer went bankrupt. Glen's brother offered him a job in Salt Lake City, Glen's hometown. After the move, Karen was put off by Glen's extended family's aggressive attempts to convert her to the Mormon faith. Glen, never really devout, became cranky, saying, "I love you; why are you so defensive and threatened by Salt Lake and my family?"

Shadows of the Past: Valerie and Tim

Valerie immigrated to the United States from South Korea with her parents and siblings when she was four, settling in a large Korean émigré community in Southern California. Tim is a doctor's son from Pennsylvania whose ethnic heritage is primarily Pennsylvania Dutch, German, and Scottish. Tim and Valerie met in college, originally drawn to each other by their many differences. As their relationship deepened they discovered that their similarities ran deeper than their differences. They reflect that comments and questions from friends and family focus on their differences, and it annoys them.

We Are More than What You See: Janette and Raul

Janette's French Canadian parents immigrated to the United States in the 1970s. Her husband, Raul, is Brazilian, with dark skin, and is often mistaken for a black American. Janette considers herself bicultural after growing up in the United States and visiting Montreal in the summers, speaking French at home and English outside the home. She says, "I am also multiethnic because I am a Jew in Seattle, Washington, where I am a minority. My husband and I consider ourselves multicultural. We think we know who we are, but trying to explain our couple identity to others is pretty crazy making."

A Sense of Place Makes the Connection: Lucy and Robert

Robert is from Nebraska and Lucy is from Iowa. They met in the US Army. They identify as multiracial but not multicultural. Robert likes to say their "culture" brought them together. "We bonded as middle-class farmers from the Midwest. I found my comfort zone with Lucy. It didn't matter that I was black and she was white. We could talk about moving back to Nebraska to farm and raise kids." According to Lucy, "In our community everyone knows and respects us. Being a biracial couple has not been a problem. Outside our community can be a different thing altogether."

First-Generation Immigrants: Gaurav and Roni

Gaurav and Roni married through a traditional family arrangement in New Delhi and immigrated to the United States in 1980. Both feel as though they belong in two places. They consider India their homeland and are committed to their children knowing extended family. Gaurev says this about the finances of traveling abroad: "Often the travel has been a financial sacrifice and meant we didn't have other kinds of family vacations. We are comfortable in both countries and sometimes not comfortable in either. Today we switch easily between customs and languages." Roni talks about feeling more comfortable with other couples who, according to her, "understand the experience of moving between two cultural worlds."

Second-Generation Immigrants: Anil and Lena

Anil is Gaurev and Roni's twenty-seven-year-old son. His fiancée is Lena, whose mother is Swedish American and whose father is from Calcutta, India, a different region altogether than the one in which Anil developed his understanding of Indian culture. Anil and Lena consider themselves multiethnic and multicultural. Anil's view on being bicultural is different from that of his parents. "I consider myself an American first, and I have a greater comfort in the US culture than that of India. I have great love for some of my Indian heritage, yet there are philosophical and cultural differences between my parents and me—the big one being marrying for love."

First- and Third-Generation Immigrants: Eric and Ling

Eric is third-generation American Chinese. Ling is a Chinese citizen and has lived in the United States for eight years. They started out as colleagues and friends at work. Their relationship became serious, and when they announced their engagement their families were thrilled. Ling says, "When we told my parents in Singapore and Eric's parents in San Francisco, they were happy to discover our family roots are from the same region of China. Everyone thought this a fortuitous sign for a happy marriage." Ling had thought she was acculturated, but in marrying an American Chinese she discovered that, in fact, she was Chinese and Eric was American. She says, "We are ethnically similar and culturally diverse."

Cultural Identity, Appearance, and Loss: Jennifer, Anders, and Hana

When Jennifer Chou married Anders Sondheim in 1982, they hyphenated their last names, content their daughter, Hana, would carry both cultural surname legacies into the world. Last year Hana married a Spaniard, Javier Garcia de Costa. Hana couldn't imagine introducing herself as Hana Chou-Sondheim-Garcia de Costa with a straight face, so she took Javier's surname. Hana also told her mother, Jennifer, that a twenty-first-century woman doesn't lose her identity by taking her husband's surname. Next month Hana and Javier are expecting their first child. Jennifer is thrilled to be a grandmother but also a little sad, remarking, "There are no sons in my generation, so there is no one left to carry on my family's surname. I also wonder if my grandbaby will look like me at all."

Social Class: Anna Maria and Eduardo

Anna Maria is first-generation Mexican American, raised by migrant farm workers. Eduardo is from an upper-class Argentine family. Family politics were a big challenge for them as early as their wedding day, when the differences in their social classes created a scene. According to Anna Maria, they had talked about eloping, but as the youngest of four kids and the only girl, she knew it would break her mother's heart. Of being shocked at the wedding, she says, "When Eduardo's extended family arrived in their fancy cars, loaded with jewelry and an entourage of nannies to mind the grandchildren, my family and friends at our little community church were upset." The couple relates that it helps when they talk about social class as being the way they are bicultural.

Join us and step back to explore the dynamics of culture, social class, social context, and family experiences that shape each partner in multicultural, multiethnic relationships. If you are in a mixed cultural, multiethnic relationship of any kind, you are the child of parents in a mixed ethnic, multicultural relationship, or you are a teacher, counselor, physician, nurse, attorney, or other type of helping professional who works with couples today, this book is for you.

HARRIET'S STORY

I grew up traveling the eastern half of the United States, experiencing regional and religious differences. Then, at midlife, I lived the expatriate life while working in South America.

The seeds of my migration journeys were planted before I was born. My parents were wrestled out of their regional comfort zones in World War II and fell in love while stationed at an army air force base in Dayton, Ohio. My mother was the granddaughter of Welsh immigrants who left the coal-mining town of Swansea, Wales and finished their lives as owners of a steel mill in the northeastern United States. My father's people, sons and daughters of the Confederacy, scrimped all their lives after surviving the double blow of the Civil War and the Great Depression. Both sets of my grandparents were fanatically loyal to their religions, social class, and politics, and not open to negotiation on any of it. My parents dealt with their in-law conflict by never living close enough to either set of parents to be expected for Sunday dinner.

In the 1950s and '60s you couldn't get from Detroit to Charleston on a freeway. Traveling from north to south, staying in small towns along the way, our accents and mannerisms softened from fast-paced metropolitan to sleepy southern, knowing without discussion how to fit in. As an adult I kept migrating, attracted to change and regional cultures without thinking about why. I lived in Missouri, California, and Rhode Island before settling in Washington State.

The experience of balancing competing world views and the expectations that accompany them drew me to study social psychology. In the 1980s, Carl Whitaker, MD, a pioneer in the field of family therapy and a mentor of mine, put my feelings into words. He used to say something like, "Every family expects loyalty to the family culture. Grandparents are forever at war with outsiders for the hearts and minds of their grandchildren." Carl made this kind of statement with a twinkle in his eye and a smile on his face, but he was deadly serious. What he meant was culture is learned. It is how you survive in the world and establish your identity; it tells you with whom and where you belong.

In my fortieth year, my family moved to Chile, where we were immersed in life and work with little preparation. I have a stack of stories on culture shock, the vulnerability of being an obvious ethnic minority, fearing for my own and my family's personal safety in rocky political environments, and struggling to get on the fast track to learn a new language. But the most emotionally charged thing was watching my children drop their American ways and integrate easily, while my husband and I were slow to find our new identities in a new culture.

Because of my time in Chile, I resonate with the complex feelings couples have struggling to keep their relationship strong and their children loyal to family values and beliefs they hold dear. As a parent who is also a therapist, I am fortunate to have more options and information than my grandparents and parents. Experience and education have taught me that to be and feel understood, you've got to keep relationship conversations up front and ongoing.

Coauthoring *Mixed Blessings* with my friend and colleague Rhoda Berlin has been a journey made with appreciation and respect for the complexity of committed relationships. Rhoda and I share similar philosophical beliefs about how cultural identity affects couple relationships at every age and stage of life while also coming at multicultural identity from our own perspectives. My hope is to share lessons learned; the insights, themes, challenges, and humor inspired by the courageous and creative multicultural, multiethnic clients with whom I have worked for nearly thirty years.

RHODA'S STORY

A wise man once told me that if he had to distill the purpose of committed relationships into one goal, it would be this: *to learn how to live with someone different from ourselves.* On a philosophical level, this says it all. Put into practice, how does that translate into action, behavior, and relationship? I've been chewing on this question ever since that long-ago conversation, both personally and professionally.

After over twenty-five years as a marriage and family therapist, I don't believe in coincidence or chance when it comes to couples' relationships. We find and choose partners for many reasons, some lying beneath the surface, even if we don't realize it at the time. So how *do* we learn to live with someone different from ourselves? Partnership requires hard work, every day. Over time as you get to know each other better, it gets easier, more natural and automatic. Building the momentum for that forward movement takes a lot of energy.

One of the most significant life lessons I ever got was delivered by a seventeen-year-old boy, just on the cusp of manhood. He said: "All I want is to be heard, understood, and accepted. Is that too much to ask?" Isn't this what we all want? Living with differences, whether visible or invisible, is all about this. It's also about hearing, understanding, and accepting ourselves so that we can do this for and with others. This requires knowing ourselves so that differences can be identified and understood from multiple perspectives. This gives us the freedom and flexibility to create alternative responses. It's all about options.

We humans usually do what comes naturally; in other words, we tend to follow Plan A, which is basically what our role models (usually our parents) did before us. Nature abhors a vacuum, so it is difficult to change this pattern unless we create new options for ourselves. Even if we want to do something different, when push comes to shove, we'll slip back into Plan A (which is what we want to change in the first place) unless we have Plans B, C, and D ready.

This is something I've lived with all my life. I watched my South Korean immigrant parents navigate their minefield of differences as they raised a family in a foreign country. To the outside world, their differences from the majority culture were very apparent. Their differences from each other were not. Those had to be experienced. As a second-generation Korean American married to a German immigrant, I've put these lessons about dealing with differences into practice. Raising three multiethnic, multicultural daughters has taught me even more. It hasn't been easy, but it has definitely been worth the struggle.

With history like this, it's no mystery why working with people from diverse backgrounds is my professional passion. This book contains my input on living interculturally, which means living with someone different from me, which is what every single person on this planet does. We are social beings; we are bonded to and through relationships.

When we first met, Harriet Cannon and I discovered that there are a lot of similarities in our differences. We've had countless conversations about how multiculturalism affects us and our clients. We train other professionals on this topic, too, so it feels natural to extend these conversations into book form. *Mixed Blessings* is written with a combined fifty-plus years of clinical experience and one-hundred-plus years of life experience. It is meant to be practical, not academic; Harriet and I are clinicians, not researchers. This book was written from the gut, based on these combined years of experiences and what we've learned from and with clients, family members, and friends.

PART ONE

.

CULTURAL UNIVERSALS

"Alike and ever alike we are on all continents in need of love, food, cloth-ing, work, speech, worship, sleep, games, dancing, fun. From tropics to the arctic humanity lives with these needs so alike, so inexorably alike."

The Family of Man
Carl Sandberg

The concept of cultural universals comes from the field of anthro-pology, but no one has evoked the sense of bonding underlying the concept better than American poet Carl Sandberg. Cultural universals are common human experiences everyone recognizes; for example, all people show affection for those they care about with a special look, a smile, a hug. All cultures have rituals such as marriage ceremonies, holiday traditions and feasts, and institu-tions for administering rules of the culture.

When people travel beyond their neighborhood or region, they frequently connect with others through cultural universals. Most of us have a story of using gestures and smiles when lost or in trouble in strange surroundings without knowing the language. Consider photojournalism, a medium where we see cultural uni-versals every day. From visuals of Olympic Games to suffering civil-ians in war-torn regions, cultural universals bring us together and open our hearts.

Cultural universals have a special position in intercultural relationships. They can remind partners about shared human values when differing expectations or cultural loyalty threaten to destroy the relationship. Love and honesty are the shared values that brought you together. The big picture can give you and your partner a balancing perspective. A conversation on cultural universals can help you and your partner sort out power struggles when each of you thinks you have the only right answer. This, in turn, can help you feel better understood and validated. The following are two brief examples of how couples used cultural universals to untangle a hot issue.

When John and Lisha met, their shared value of having a spiritual practice drew them together and strengthened their relationship. John was a Christian and Lisha was a Buddhist. They could talk philosophically about the meaning of religion in their lives with mutual enthusiasm for their partner's beliefs. They were content to practice as they believed until the birth of their first child, after which time John's and Lisha's different practices became a painful conflict. At first, they argued about which spiritual practice would take the lead in the child's upbringing. Then they remembered their shared value of spirituality was a major factor that bound their relationship. Appreciating that spirituality is a universal, they were able to detach from the idea of being "right" and work through the intense feelings of wanting one way to prevail. They could look at compromises that were honest and ongoing. It took time and tears, but eventually they agreed to go forward.

Emilia and Mark were planning their wedding while living in New Jersey, three thousand miles from their families in Los Angeles. Emilia had a large extended family with a tradition of spending whatever it took regardless of taking on significant debt. Mark was the only child of a single mother and wanted a small, quiet ceremony with the immediate family and a few friends.

They talked to their parents about the big-picture meaning of marriage. Emilia and Mark's solution was a small wedding at a beautiful park and a big party reception in Emilia's neighborhood the following day. Both families were affirmed. Emilia and Mark were able to nondefensively look at their first cross-cultural challenge using cultural universals as a mediator. Spending time on the big picture worked for this couple. Once they got away from conflict and focused on the universal joy of the marriage celebration, they could smooth parental hurt feelings and honor both families.

Using cultural universals to solve a family problem is not a panacea. Individuals in either or both families may not be happy, but it will set the tone for how a couple can honor traditions creatively in the future.

For a broader picture of the breadth and depth of cultural universals, take a look at the list of examples in this chapter. You will most likely find specific cultural universals toward which you resonate as a couple. When you run into conflict and target the basic cultural universal involved, it will be easier to find some common ground. Then you can deconstruct the problem with more confidence and clarity.

CULTURAL UNIVERSALS LIST

A cultural universal is an element, pattern, trait, or institution that is common in some form to all human cultures past and present worldwide.

age-related roles
annual calendar
athletic sports
bodily adornment
community organization
cooking rules
cooperative labor
cosmology
courtship
dancing
decorative art
division of labor
dream interpretation
education
ethics
etiquette
faith healing
family
feasting
fire making
family roles

inheritance rules
joking
kinship groups
kinship relationship names
language
laws
luck, superstitions
magic
marriage
mealtimes
medicine
modesty about natural functions
mourning
music
mythology
numerals, number system
obstetrics
personal names
penalties for breaking the law
population control
postnatal care

folklore	property rights
food taboos	puberty and rites of passage
funerals	religious ritual
games	sexual restrictions
gestures	soul concepts
gift giving	status differentiation
government	surgery
greetings	tool making
hairstyles	trade
hospitality	visiting friends, family
housing	weaning infants
hygiene training	weather understanding, control
incest taboos	

Adapted from the work of George P. Murdock, "The Common Denominator of Cultures" chart, first published in *The Science of Man in World Crisis*, Columbia University Press, 1945.

COLLECTIVIST AND INDIVIDUALIST CULTURES

The structure of our culture holds us together psychologically just as our skeletons and muscles hold our bodies together physically. Fortunately, culture is learned, not inherited, which gives us options for change we could never make with our physical bodies.

It would take a lifetime to describe the nuances of every culture and subculture. Our purpose in this chapter is to talk generally about the structure of collectivist and individualist cultures, note some hallmarks of each, and leave you to ponder where the differences between them impact your relationship.

Teasing out whether you are more collectivist or individualist can be a subtle exercise in the twenty-first century. Globalization and technology have made us appear more homogeneous today than even ten years ago. But if you look beyond the trappings of the modern world to basic philosophical beliefs about how relationships function, many differences emerge.

Deconstructing a culture is complicated; therefore, this chapter also includes graphics illustrating the basic workings of collectivist

9

and individualist cultures. After looking at the charts, you might want to reread this section and pull it all together. A list of books with more information on collectivist and individualist cultures appears in our resource section.

Collectivist Cultures

Collectivist cultures make up the world's majority cultural orientation. All of Asia, the Indian subcontinent, most of Africa, Central and South America, Mexico, and parts of Eastern Europe are generally considered collectivist cultures.

Collectivist structure evolved around the world as large family groups settled the land. To sustain an agrarian lifestyle without modern equipment required a high degree of collaboration in close quarters. Family groups sought harmony through well-defined gender roles and hierarchy. People avoided overt conflict in relationships because every person's labor was needed for the survival of the group.

Another way to look at the structure of collectivist culture is to compare it to an elite military group such as the US Navy SEALs. Both are groups that are hierarchical and deeply relational. Expectations for responsibilities and loyalty are not left to creative interpretation. Everyone has a position, a job, a role, and each person knows his impact on group success without needing reminders.

Collectivist cultures are high context. That means the culture's nuances are transmitted very subtly and information on how things work is not written down in a manual. Like the Navy SEALs, the rules are clear and people don't need reminders. The subtlety of rules in a high-context culture makes moving or marrying into a collectivist culture difficult for individualists.

Collectivist children learn through observation how relationships work. The well-being of the family is everyone's priority; for example, a sister and her husband will contribute to the college fund of an older brother's talented son even if it means their own child may miss out in the short term. The talented nephew will then be obligated to help his aunt's children or grandchildren in return. The hierarchy is entrenched and reliable, and family members have faith it will continue to work for them.

Collectivist cultures are polychronic. In other words, time is not precise; it just flows. For example, living in the flow and nourishing close relationships is more important than being timely. If Paulo is running late on his way to his dentist and runs into his second cousin whom he hasn't seen in a month, Paulo will stop to visit regardless of his being late. When he arrives at the dentist's office and tells her what happened, she, another collectivist, will understand and not be upset.

Collectivists tend to be patient regarding life circumstances in a way that may seem fatalistic to individualists. Philosophically, collectivists are inclined to have acceptance, tolerance, and a certain pride about their inherited social standing. It is likely you will die a member of the same social class into which you were born. Change happens, but not easily, and there is a certain dignity given to membership in all social classes.

Collectivists appreciate the natural environment and don't try to manipulate the setting in which they live just because they can. They are more inclined to be at peace with the natural world even if it is uncomfortable. They are slow and careful in making social connections, alignments, and relationships. They pay acute attention to nuances in the environment and take advantage of possibilities when they arise. This pays off because the benefits of the family's support, pride, and opportunities come to the individual or her descendants in time. The valuable rewards for personal sacrifice are support, respect, and belonging.

Individualist Cultures

In today's world, individualist cultures are the minority cultural structure. The regions with classic individualist cultures are Western Europe, the British Isles, Canada, the United States, Australia, and New Zealand.

Individualist cultural structure evolved in Western Europe in the 1700s, around the time of the Industrial Revolution. Individuals were leaving the family community and moving off the land to live and work in cities. Concurrently, the Protestant Reformation in Europe emphasized personal responsibility, including hard work, social service, and charity, as the way into God's grace. This new interpretation of living a righteous life encouraged individual achievement and rewarded individual excellence. Public schools, charities, and government social services evolved as safety nets when extended families were not available.

From a broad philosophical standpoint, individualist cultures have characteristics similar to John Wayne in the Western movies genre from the 1950s and 1960s. John, the stereotypical cowboy, believes in romantic love yet is fiercely independent. He is straightforward and direct, and considers others to be of questionable trustworthiness when they have a different communication style.

Freedom to make personal decisions is expected and considered nonnegotiable. Living apart from the support of extended family, John has learned to rely on his intuition and creativity. He relishes hard work and competition and will strive tirelessly to win the day. John's self-reliance has taught him to have marginal regard for hierarchy. He is, however, fiercely loyal to loved ones and will follow a leader to protect them or to protect an ideal he honors, such as democracy. In conclusion, independence, freedom of expression and creativity are valued more by our cowboy than conforming to what a group or family or society expects.

The United States is primarily a country of immigrants who came from many cultures speaking diverse languages. In the early days the grueling travel across oceans and land meant people left their homeland alone, never to see their families again. Because of the cost and physical danger, extended family groups rarely immigrated together. In order to survive people had to develop personal competence, embrace change, and cooperate with strangers. America's Founding Fathers, many of whom came from families that immigrated to the New World to escape religious persecution and European class prejudice, wrote egalitarian, individualist values into the United States Constitution and Bill of Rights.

Individualist cultures are low context. That means for the sake of efficiency, equality, and clarity, rules are explicit and available to everybody. Individualist parents and school systems train children to follow explicit rules for good citizenship and performance. Directions are generally well marked and clear, with graphics and written language. Interpreters are available for the deaf, and braille is in places such as elevators and public restrooms. Maps and street signs are accurate and available so that travelers can find their way alone. Individualists talk about balancing challenges; for instance, fairness versus competition and adaptability versus tradition. Meanwhile, they maintain cooperation, and rule following exists to benefit both the individual and society.

Individualist cultures are monochronic. Being on time is important. In a culture where logic, efficiency, and hard work are hallmarks of cultural values, it is considered rude to keep anyone, regardless of position in society, waiting. Let's take Sue as an example. She was caught in traffic and arrived thirty minutes late for her haircut. The stylist, whom Sue had known several years, was apologetic when she told Sue they'd have to reschedule. To keep the appointment would disrupt the rest of the stylist's afternoon schedule, and that was unacceptable.

Individualists want equality, so while social classes exist, achieving higher status usually comes through personal achievement rather than family connections or tradition. This belief in hard work, personal responsibility, and giving on behalf of those less fortunate has led individualistic cultures to be aggressive in changing the physical environment for the betterment of the individual and society. Bridges, freeways, and schools are built with benefit in mind for all, not just the elite. Individualists believe in solving problems promptly. People in individualist cultures debate long-term social and economic planning, yet individualists do not have a patient culture.

Collectivist and individualist cultures each have strengths and challenges. As you look at the charts and read the keys on collectivist and individualist cultures, you may find that you identify with some parts of both. Ask yourself which parts resonate with you. You might find it interesting to look at the cultural heritages of your parents and grandparents to shed light on ways in which you identify with collectivist or individualist structures. You might also consider going to the Your Ethnic Heritage exercise in the resource section to add to the conversation on how you identify.

Collectivist Culture

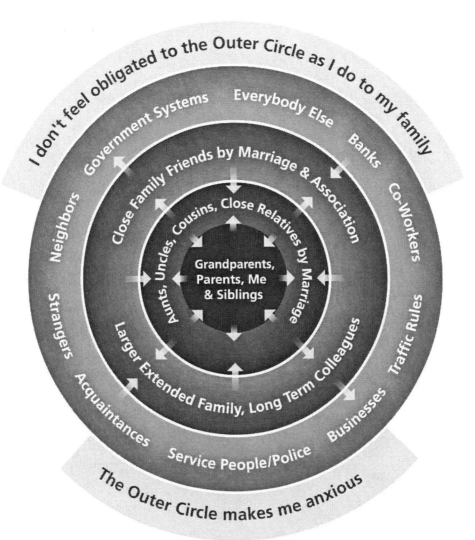

I don't feel obligated to the Outer Circle as I do to my family

Everybody Else

Government Systems

Banks

Neighbors

Close Family Friends by Marriage & Association

Co-Workers

Aunts, Uncles, Cousins, Close Relatives by Marriage

Strangers

Grandparents, Parents, Me & Siblings

Traffic Rules

Larger Extended Family, Long Term Colleagues

Businesses

Acquaintances

Service People/Police

The Outer Circle makes me anxious

COLLECTIVIST
CULTURE GRAPHIC

(moving from the innermost circle outward)

The Innermost Circles:
The innermost circles are the inner sanctum of the immediate family. Extended family members in the second circle are loyal and trusted. The arrows in the graphic show the permeable boundary between the two circles, meaning we have frequent extended family contact and tight relationships. As family we are interdependent and cooperative in helping each other get things done. As individuals we give and receive lifelong loyalty and adhere to family hierarchy and roles. Individual success is considered family success just as individual failure is considered family shame.

The Third Circle:
The boundaries between the second and third circles are less permeable. We nourish our third circle relationships. When we need a plumber, insurance agent, or banker, we look to this circle for trusted connections and recommendations. Relationships with these people are sustained for generations. For example, Paulo, whose grandfather started the business, may not be the best insurance agent in town, but our relationship loyalty means he will give us good service and a fair deal. When he or one of his

family members needs help, we will return the favor. That's how the world works in collectivist cultures.

The Fourth Circle:

We don't trust strangers or institutions. They aren't safe relationships. Notice that the permeability in and out of the fourth circle is restricted. Whenever possible we interact with schools, health care, businesses, and government only through trusted generations-long relationships in the first three circles. From a collectivist perspective, these connections assure that things get done. Who you know matters more than how competent you are at what you do.

Individualist Culture

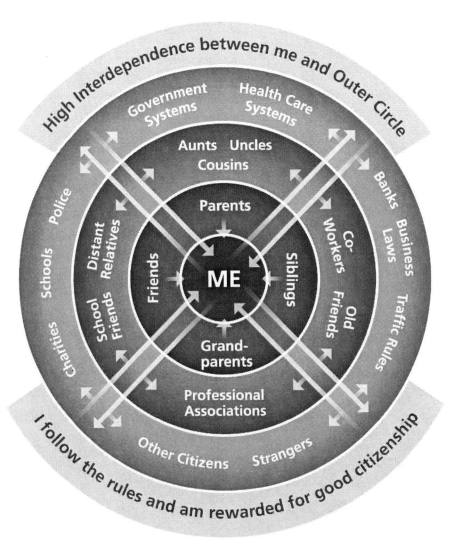

INDIVIDUALIST
CULTURE GRAPHIC

(moving from the innermost circle outward)

The Innermost Circle:

I am the center of my life. My life's goal is to be the very best person I can be. My goal and my family's goal for me is to self-actualize, trust myself, and be a strong, independent person. That means working hard, being creative, thinking outside the box, following laws, paying taxes, being charitable to strangers, and helping take care of those less fortunate than myself. You can see from the arrows that once I reach adulthood, the first place I will look if I need help is government and civil institutions set up to provide specific services.

The Second Circle:

The second circle nurtures me as a child. Family and friends are very important while I am young. The relationship arrows pass through this circle on their path outward. As I grow, my family will encourage and mentor me to become independent, expecting me to set up my own household and support myself whether or not I marry. As an adult I may be close to my family if our personalities are compatible, but if not, I feel no strong cultural obligation to be emotionally close to them or to support them financially.

The Third Circle:

Different people in the third circle will be important to me at different times in my life. The arrows show a circular pattern of extended family, friends, mentors, and colleagues who come and go as I grow from childhood to adulthood. Depending on my personality, the third circle could include just a few or even hundreds of people who are acquaintances I don't see anymore, or rarely see but were close to at one time. An example of this is my "friends" on Facebook.

The Outermost Circle:

There is a high degree of interaction and interdependence between the outermost circle and me. The arrows show connection and permeability. My self-expectation is to work hard, be creative, be successful in my chosen work, and follow the cultural rules. This entitles me to partake freely of the public services and institutions my taxes and government provide. In general I trust these institutions to educate my children and take care of me if I am ill or elderly. I vote, volunteer, and work to make the schools, health care systems, police, and other social systems the best they can be. Participating in the systems is my responsibility as a citizen.

ACCULTURATION

Acculturation is a main task for people who make a major move. We all in our own ways experience and react to the losses, gains, challenges, and joys of being in a new country. Acculturation is the process by which we familiarize ourselves in new surroundings, with the ultimate goal of finding or making a place for ourselves in a new society. It's about finding ways to feel like we belong. It's about building a new sense of community and home. In other words, it's figuring out how to fit in. Those that study the phenomenon say this process can take years, even decades. Some people, depending on their age at immigration, never feel like they belong. Some don't ever want to.

Acculturation stories can have profound, generations-long effects on our relationships. Have you ever felt dumbfounded by how your family operates? If you investigate your family's migration and acculturation story, you may find the reason. How a family deals with acculturation can result in traditions and legacies that dictate how we cope with adversity, problem solve, and communicate. It can also lead to holes in what later generations know and understand about their family because, especially in families that lived through traumatic experiences, family secrets often arise.

Migration and acculturation add another layer of complication to the cultural identity mix. How a person acculturates depends on gender, social class, education, social environment, and values. Personality traits, familial or community expectations, and their accompanying pressures are also factors.

Acculturation Process

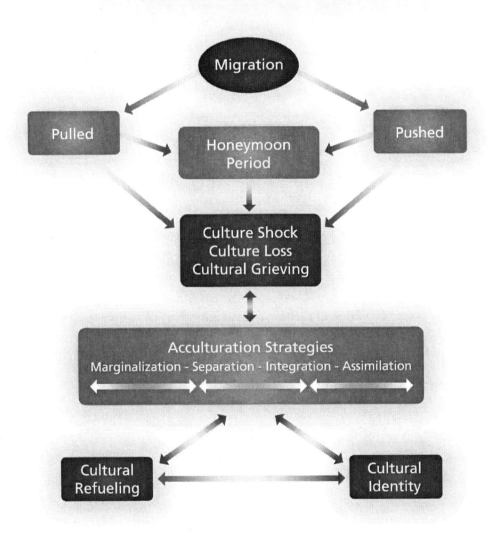

Let's look at the acculturation process in a broad sense by going over the graphic.

Migration

- An individual or family relocation is the starting point of acculturation.
- Moving to a different region of the same country can be as impactful as moving internationally.

Pulled and/or Pushed

- When we're pulled the move is usually a response to an opportunity, such as education, a job prospect, or a relationship.
- When we're pushed it is usually a response to some catastrophe, such as economic hardship, war, or persecution.

Honeymoon Period

- There's so much to explore! Everything is exciting; there are new opportunities and people are welcoming and helpful; strangers wave.
- Optimism reigns. What's not to love? We're so glad we came!

Culture Shock, Culture Loss, and Cultural Grieving

- Things aren't as wonderful as they first seemed. We realize that people have been waving at us with only one particular finger, not the whole hand as we're used to back home, and now we know what that waving finger means.
- Homesickness sets in. We miss familiar smells, flavors, clothes, and sounds that helped us know who we are. We're not sure where we fit in this new society.

- Losses must be mourned. Healthy grieving aids the acculturation process, helping us adapt to our new environment. This can be difficult when the expectation is that we must be grateful to be in this new place. Such pressure can add to the sense of being alone.

Acculturation Strategies:

John W. Berry of Queens University in Ontario, Canada developed this fourfold model.

- **Marginalization:** We feel disconnected from both our old and new cultures. We try to fit in with our immigrant compatriots but are unsuccessful. We try to make inroads with members of the majority culture but feel rejected. We feel alone and adrift, without a culture. Marginalization is the situation that can be most problematic, since we are a social species and have a strong need to bond and belong. Feeling rejected or outcast can lead us to reject others as a way of protecting ourselves from hurt feelings and bruised egos.
- **Separation:** The pain of leaving home is overwhelming, so we do our best to recreate what we left behind. We arrange our lives so we don't have to learn the new language. Examples of this can be found in ethnic enclaves such as Chinatown or Little Italy in major urban areas. Unfortunately, when we choose this strategy, it can cause misunderstandings, especially between us and the majority culture.
- **Assimilation:** Seen in the past as the ultimate goal of acculturation, assimilation is when we rapidly abandon our original culture and submerge ourselves in the new culture. Examples of this are anglicizing our names and ceasing to speak our mother tongues in favor of speaking only the majority culture's language, preferably without an accent.

- **Integration:** This is currently seen as the most beneficial acculturation strategy for both us and society. In this scenario we select elements from both our home and new cultures to build a life compatible with our values and world view. An example of this is a family educating their daughters despite their home culture's disapproval. In turn, the larger community actively embraces the influences imported by its newest citizens, an example being multiple ethnic eateries on the same street, each filled by a diverse clientele.

Cultural Refueling

- Refilling the void is one proactive, joyful way of dealing with culture loss. Migrants get their heritage "fix" through cultural refueling: Ana left the Southwest. Her mother regularly sends her culinary care packages including chipotle chili powder with just the right amount of smoky heat. Dave spent his adolescence surfing and is now landlocked. His favorite way to unwind is by watching the surfing film *Endless Summer*. You miss Delhi, so you make samosas with friends while listening to Bollywood CDs.

Cultural Identity

- Forming a clear sense of identity is a goal of acculturation.

Let's put all of this together in one family's multigenerational migration and acculturation story. Meet the Kozlowski clan:

Tobiasz and Brygida Kozlowski left Poland for the United States of America in 1986. Tobiasz had been a journalist who sneaked articles and photos out of the country during the tense years when citizens were taking an active stand against the Communist government.

Tobiasz knew it was only a matter of time before he was arrested, so a network of allies arranged for him and his family to leave. At the time Tobiasz and Brygida were thirty-eight. They had three children: Dominik (fourteen), Pawla (eleven), and Wit (six).

They moved to Milwaukee, Wisconsin, which has a large Polish community. They were happy to be there, yet regretted leaving Brygida's parents behind. Tobiasz taught journalism. Brygida, a mathematics teacher in Poland, worked hard on her English and eventually went into real estate, mostly catering to the Polish community. Tobiasz and Brygida dealt with the outside world when they had to, but the cornerstone of their lives was family and community.

The children, however, had different acculturation experiences. They attended public schools where most of their peers were Americans of European heritage whose families had been in the United States for generations. These classmates were, as Pawla put it, "typical white bread." Dominik, the oldest sibling, had been outgoing in Poland, but in the United States he became withdrawn. Attending English as a Second Language classes carried a stigma, and as a result he and Pawla were labeled FOBs (fresh off the boats). Whereas Pawla sought acceptance from non-Polish peers, Dominik only socialized with fellow Polish Americans. Pawla practiced English with her parents and changed the spelling of her name to Paula.

Wit (pronounced Veet) started the first grade with a good working knowledge of English. By the time he was in third grade he spoke perfect English, while his Polish remained at a six-year-old level. His elementary school years were fairly low stress; nonetheless, kids made fun of his name. By middle school the bullying heightened and he became depressed. One year for Christmas he asked to switch schools and change his name. He received both and completed middle school in joyful anonymity with a first name of his choosing: William, Will for short.

Brygida's parents, Miroslaw and Kornelia, had joined the family in the United States in 1991. When they arrived Miroslaw was seventy-four and Kornelia sixty-nine. They were overwhelmed by the vastness of space and number of choices America offered. Over time they limited their exposure to this confusion by developing a comforting daily routine consisting of walks within a ten-block radius of the house. They stopped at a Polish cafe for lunch, read a local Polish language newspaper, and reminisced about home. Neither learned English, as they had no need for it. This caused awkwardness with Paula and Will, who resisted speaking Polish. It also caused conflict with Brygida and Tobiasz, whom the grand-parents felt should be raising their children to be proud Poles.

After attending the University of Wisconsin, Dominik got a mas-ter's degree in business administration at a university in Cracow, Poland, where he met and married Adela. He got a job with an American firm that did business in Poland and spent time in both countries. When Adela became pregnant with their first child, they settled in Warsaw.

Meanwhile, Paula became a nurse and, much to her parents' cha-grin, lived in an apartment in another part of Milwaukee. Her parents wanted her to live at home to help care for her aging grandparents. Paula married Gustavo Ortiz, a public relations professional of Puerto Rican heritage. Tobiasz and Brygida were displeased their daughter married a non-Pole. However, Gus was raised Catholic in a collectivist culture, so Paula's parents could relate to him at that level. They were eventually able to develop a cordial relationship; nonetheless, when Gus was offered a transfer to another state, he and Paula made the move.

Will attended the University of Michigan, which surprised his parents, who had assumed he'd attend the University of Wisconsin like his siblings. By the time he graduated he had reduced visits home to holidays, weddings, and funerals. By the age of thirty he was phoning home for holidays, preferring to spend them with his girlfriend Linda's family, whom he considered "Heinz 57 American."

When Paula and Gus's second daughter was born, the baptism was held at the Kozlowskis' church with Will as the baby's godfather. The celebration brought the entire family together for the first time in several years. His older brother Dominik's strong Polish identity was not surprising to Will, but seeing Paula slide back into Polish ways was disconcerting. When Will's girlfriend, Linda, expressed admiration for his family's strong traditions and tight-knit community, Will felt a different kind of shock. He recognized how pleased he was at Linda's reaction and realized he might be a proud Pole after all. After that he set out to reconnect with his family and heritage more thoroughly.

Things to Consider:

- Do you identify with any parts of the acculturation story and challenges from the Kozlowski family story?

- What do you know about your own family's migration story? Complete the Your Ethnic Heritage exercise in the resource section.

LIFE STAGES AND CULTURE

To everything (turn, turn, turn)
There is a season (turn, turn, turn)
And a time to every purpose
under heaven.

Pete Seeger
(Adapted from the book of Ecclesiastes)

Libraries are full of books that describe human development at each phase of life. We are adding yet another chapter. Here we explore life stages and how understanding their universality across cultures, subcultures, and ethnicities can benefit couple relationships. Much of the chronology of life stages as we present them stems from the work of Erik Erikson, a multicultural, multilingual pioneer in the field of psychosocial development. Although Erikson published his book *Childhood and Society* in the midtwentieth century, his concepts continue to be respected for their clarity and culturally neutral language. A recommendation for more about Erik Erikson can be found in the resource section.

We believe couples' conversations about life growing up can be invaluable. Comparing what happened at different stages, including acculturation challenges, can bring couples to a deeper understanding of each other. We've heard couples bemoan the need to work on yet another facet of their relationship. They express their desire to deal with the here and now, not the past. Our response is always the same: Yes, it's a lot of work. Nonetheless, multicultural couples that do this work are more likely to be supportive partners who understand one another with less hurtful judgment.

In addition to the tasks and goals for every life stage usually found in such developmental charts, our table includes potential acculturation challenges. These challenges are possible roadblocks that people must navigate while transitioning to life in a new culture or subculture. It's also important to note that when we talk about life stages and acculturation challenges, we have a liberal interpretation that includes regional as well as international migrations and transitions.

Our interpretation encompasses experiences of individuals and families who go from being majority members of their community to being minority members of a new community. We also focus on the role of strong relationships at each stage. We acknowledge that adolescence and young adulthood arrive earlier in agrarian or less developed countries, and the boundaries between young adulthood and middle adulthood in individuals from urban areas or developed countries vary.

Here are three couples who used stories about their developmental life stages and acculturation challenges to deepen their relationship connection. Take a look at the chart and consider how the following examples may be similar to some of your own experiences.

Rose emigrated from the Philippines with her family to Portland, Oregon, when she was eight. When she was thirty she got engaged to Richard, a third-generation Filipino American. Because Rose immigrated so young and seemed so American, they both initially downplayed the fact that she was indeed foreign born. It wasn't until they spent quality time telling stories from different ages and stages of their lives that Richard could emotionally resonate to the trauma Rose experienced being an outsider at a stage of life where being like everyone else seemed like the most important thing in the world. Their aha moment happened when Rose revealed a poignant memory of lunchtime in the third grade. Every morning her mother packed lunches her friends called smelly. Rose soon decided that rather than expose herself to the ridicule of being different, she would throw her lunches away. She went hungry at school for weeks. Her teacher eventually discovered her secret, but rather than expose Rose to embarrassment, the teacher introduced Rose to the cupboard where she kept bread and peanut butter. Thereafter, Rose made her own daily sandwich.

All countries have subcultures, yet it still comes as a surprise when stories show a regional migration to be as hard as any immigration experience. Appreciation of the effects of a regional transition often don't hit home until adulthood.

When Nancy was fourteen her father's promotion moved them from rural Ohio to suburban Los Angeles. They left behind their extended family, community, and cultural touchstones. It was a rocky few months for everybody, but her father loved his new job and her mother learned to entertain, and the couple enjoyed exploring the region. Her younger brothers, who were eight and ten, became involved with sports and were Southern Californians overnight. Nancy was different. She pined for her grandmother and cousins and the close family lifestyle in Ohio. Years later when Nancy and Mario started dating, one thing that brought them closer was discussing the importance of extended family relationships and a place to be rooted. Nancy got validation for her loss of family and cultural community from Mario's mother and grandmother. Nancy and Mario joke that the close-knit rural families of Ohio and central valley California never would have guessed they had so much in common.

Cultures evolve organically. When people move away, they aren't there to observe gradual changes in their culture of origin.

They may be very shocked when they return to visit and are confronted with the differences. Sharing stories about birth culture experiences at different stages can help couples understand culture loss when it affects the relationship.

Ashane left Sri Lanka for Canada at age twenty and didn't return until he and his wife, Sandra, made a visit during Sandra's pregnancy twelve years later. They were both excited to experience places Ashane knew as a child. In Ashane's mind Sri Lanka had remained the same, but in reality it had, of course, changed. Much of what Ashane remembered was gone. When they returned to Canada, Ashane became depressed. For a while the visit undermined Ashane's confidence in becoming the kind of father he had envisioned himself to be. Ashane and Sandra found it helpful to talk about the universal needs of babies. Later they discussed specific cultural parts they would mix from Sri Lanka and Canada to raise their child in a mutually satisfying style.

Things to Consider:

- Find the developmental stage where you fit today and talk about the expectations you received at home for your current life stage.

- How smoothly did family transitions go when you were growing up? Were there family illnesses or financial or marital problems that caused stress? Some families don't talk about family issues or adversity. You may have to do your research in carefully worded ways to get useful answers to fill out your family history if you don't know it.

- If you are moving into a different life stage than where you were when you became a couple, how are you talking about your expectations for this next phase of life?

Developmental Life Stages

Developmental Stage and Goal	Important Relationships	Important Tasks	Acculturation Challenges
Infancy *Learning to trust*	Mother and father, grandparents	To receive consistent love and care	Distracted, stressed parents are overwhelmed by migration or cultural adjustments.
Toddlerhood *Gaining control of one's physical body*	Parents and close family who teach loving, clear limits	Learning to control body and bodily functions	Conflicting cultural practices confuse the child and undermine confidence.
Preschool Years *Taking initiative*	Family mentors child in positive ways; outside influences enter	Confidence to explore the environment, play, socialize	Missed cultural cues cause problems at play and elsewhere. Parents may resist outside influences.
School Age *Making things, cooperating in-groups*	A safe, stimulating neighborhood and school	To work hard, cooperate, be part of the group	Conflict arises between the desire to conform and loyalty to the family. There can be shame about being different.
Adolescence *Meaningful self-identity*	Positive role models and peer groups	To become oneself, share of oneself, develop loyalty	Family values vs. peer group/dominant culture values create identity confusion and undermine self-esteem.
Young Adult *Intimate relationships*	Close friends, community, spouse or life partner	Successful relationships, love, and fidelity	Clarification of cultural identity is essential for emotional intimacy.
Middle Adult *Community/world involvement*	Family group, parenthood, career mentorship	To create and make things that outlast you; care for others	Developing meaningful connections prevents self-centeredness.
Older Adult *Personal integrity*	The interconnections of community and humankind	To freely give philosophical guidance; to reflect on life's meaning	Integration of life experience is necessary to prevent bitterness or depression due to focusing on life's disappointments.

ETHNOCENTRISM

*"We make a rational assumption about someone's behavior based on what we would, or would not, do in the same circumstances, ignoring the **otherness of the other**. We consider only influences that make us what we are and impose those beliefs on them." [Emphasis added]*

The Dying Light
Henry Porter

Valerie and Tim's first Christmas together as a married couple was approaching. Their previous Christmases had been spent apart because as college students each had returned to his or her parents' home for winter break. Valerie, the second-generation Korean American mentioned in our introduction, expected Tim to be excited about the prospect of being in sunny California over the winter holiday. Tim, the Pennsylvania Dutch doctor's son, expected Valerie to be excited about experiencing her first "white Christmas" in Pennsylvania. When they finally got around to talking about it, each was perplexed and more than a little resentful that his or her partner wasn't willing to spend the holiday with the in-laws. Each had assumed the other would want to share and adopt a treasured holiday experience, a piece of his or her partner's heritage, tradition, and cultural identity. Each was surprised and hurt by the other's reluctance to give up his or her family's practice. It was their first big fight and it stung. The holidays were supposed to bring them closer together, not highlight their differences.

This was *ethnocentrism* at work. Ethnocentrism is not racism. An ethnocentric perspective means we consider what we know to be best. It's rooting for the New York Yankees instead of the Texas Rangers. Here is our practical definition:

> Ethnocentrism is the belief that my ethnic, regional, or cultural group is of the greatest importance. I use my group as the standard against which I compare all others. The most common areas of comparison are language, customs, socially appropriate behavior, and spiritual practices.

Ethnocentrism is a natural human phenomenon with key evolutionary purposes. It is an integral part of the development of our cultural identities. When the human species was young, survival depended on knowing where and with whom we belonged. It was vital to be able to quickly gauge the level of risk posed by strangers.

We still identify and categorize other people. It helps us identify our "in-group" or "tribe" and create our safety zone. Think of sayings we have along these lines:

> *Birds of a feather flock together.*
> *If it looks like a duck and quacks like a duck, it's a duck.*

Think about the last time you asked a stranger for the time. How did you choose someone to approach? You probably looked for someone wearing a watch or carrying a cell phone. Did you also consider his or her dress, demeanor, gender, age, or ethnicity? This is natural, automatic, and usually unconscious. We judge appearances to minimize our risk of harm and maximize our chance of success.

Today's political landscape attempts to be bias free. We like to think that physical appearance has little to do with how we relate to people. Recent brain research shows this isn't true. Human beings have an evolutionary need to identify with groups. Part of the process of recognizing our in-group is governed by an older part of our brains, the amygdala.

The amygdala governs the fight-or-flight survival reflex. It constantly scans our environment for potential danger. When it comes to choosing whom we spend time with, our amygdala influences our initial reactions to new people. It helps us identify potential members of our in-group while also alerting us to outsiders. Visual familiarity speaks of community, unspoken understanding, and instant connection. Ethnocentrism in this form is about this sense of safety, comfort, and, most of all, belonging.

Anyone who survived the teen years knows exactly what in-groups and out-groups are. We all want to belong, and we each have to develop our own definition of what that means and how it affects our behavior. Luckily, we are not solely dependent on the more primitive parts of our brains. Our frontal cortex enables critical thinking. If we react negatively to a stranger based on appearances, it's up to us to remind ourselves to override our fight-or-flight instincts.

Tim and Valerie were not the only ones in their families who had to redefine belonging. In addition to the differences between their East and West Coast cultures, they were the first multiethnic couple in either family. This forced their family members to redefine their tribes, since there was now a member who looked like he or she didn't belong.

Another sensitive topic was how they each responded to strangers' reactions to them. When people stared, Tim got mad. Valerie ignored looks and comments. She got upset at Tim's reactions and wished he would relax. Valerie's motto was: "Don't give them power over you. Otherwise they win." This only fueled Tim's anger.

Valerie's ethnocentric thinking, based on her collectivist perspective, affected her coping strategies, meaning that it was shameful to show a response to strangers' behaviors. Tim's ethnocentric thinking, based on his individualist approach, shaped his responses as well. For him, it was all-important to stand up for his wife and himself. Once they figured out what was going on, they no longer took what was happening personally. That made it a lot easier to work together to make changes.

Things to Consider:

- The first step in resolving conflict is being able to clearly identify it. If you identify arguments based on ethnocentric thinking, you're already a step ahead. A tool you can use to explore the sources of this thinking is the Culturegram. It is designed to help you develop a different relationship with your attitudes and actions. Tim and Valerie's Culturegrams are in the resource section as models.

- Many people of European heritage whose families have been in the United States three or more generations have little if any information about their cultural roots and traditions. This is true because the "melting pot" value of fitting in that began in the nineteenth century and lasted into the end of the twentieth century merged into an Anglo-American identity that had no cultural edges. How do you relate to this statement?

CODESWITCHING

Codeswitching emerged from the field of linguistics and has spread into the mainstream. The main concept of codeswitching is using multiple languages or communication styles to transition smoothly between cultures and subcultures in your environment. For instance, we use a different tone and cadence when talking with our three-year-old versus our mother. Our language choices when communicating with a professional colleague are different than those we use with our best friend.

Most of the time, adjusting language to ages and stages is intuitive and effortless, requiring little thought. At other times codeswitching can be intellectually jarring—for instance, when someone struggles to learn a language and tries to participate in a new culture.

Consider John, who may become frustrated if he travels to Mexico and expects to get along on his high school Spanish. Let's say he becomes lost. While asking a local woman for help, he translates her Spanish into English in his head. Then he generates an appropriate English response and translates this into Spanish. Meanwhile, the Spanish speaker has continued her side of the conversation and John has lost the flow. They are lost in the codeswitching gap and are both frustrated.

Sometimes codeswitching is inconvenient. It is often funny. Thankfully, it is rarely tragic. In multicultural relationships codeswitching gaps tend to ebb and flow. When a couple is feeling connected, small codeswitching miscommunications that cause confusion or frustration are easy to catch. Eventually couples become so attuned to each other that codeswitching is easy and natural. They recognize when a partner is having a bad day, is lonely, or is homesick, and don't take little pricks or irritations personally. Now imagine John and the Spanish speaking woman are a committed couple. Their frustration takes on a new intensity because more is at stake.

In very stressful times the most fluent codeswitcher can unravel. Illness, stress at work, visits with relatives, marital conflict, or just about any unexpected life circumstance can bring on a lapse. When communication gets rough for one or both partners, it's time to talk.

Consider Klaus, from Austria, and Lisa, born and raised in the United States. Klaus had worked in the United States five years before they married. He considered himself bilingual and bicultural. Lisa enjoyed vacationing in Austria with Klaus's family. She felt embraced by the culture although she wasn't fluent in German. When Klaus's father died unexpectedly, Klaus and Lisa took bereavement leave and stayed on in Austria. Klaus became short tempered and retreated into his native culture. He had trouble tracking in-depth conversations with Lisa in English. Lisa felt hurt and frustrated at not being able to comfort Klaus in his grief. It took some time for this couple to realize that in addition to being affected by grief, Klaus's codeswitching facility disappeared with the shock of the sudden loss.

To alleviate such misunderstandings, most couples find it imperative to risk being vulnerable with each other when they feel misunderstood. For instance, things improved when Lisa was able to talk about her feelings of helplessness in the face of Klaus's suffering, and Klaus was able to find the words to talk about his pain.

During challenging emotional moments bilingual couples need to remember that problems with language are different than problems caused by insensitivity. Taking time to problem solve and get the words right makes all the difference.

Accuracy in codeswitching is not only switching back and forth between languages. It's related to having a deep understanding of both cultures, including those concepts that can't be translated. It takes patience and a good sense of humor, and even then you can lose your cool.

Anna Maria and Eduardo, whom we met in the Introduction, bonded as immigrants. They acknowledged they were raised with different cultural world views but nonetheless fell into the trap of minimizing their differences. Anna Maria was from a farming community in Mexico, and Eduardo was the son of a surgeon in Buenos Aires. They were successful in sensitively blending their cultures, and yet their bliss unraveled whenever family from either side visited.

Anna Maria and Eduardo's solution was to develop a personal code signaling when each needed a time out. Anna Maria would wipe her brow; Eduardo would blow his nose. Once this plan was established, it was agreed they would talk about the issue later, but for now, move on. They came to understand they could switch between cultures without becoming defensive when extended family came to town.

Individuals offer unique talents. Some learn new languages quickly, while others need more time. One person might embrace a new culture, while his or her partner requires more energy for the process. When partners talk about codeswitching and communicate when they feel misunderstood, it is easier to close the codeswitching gap. Risking mutual vulnerability leads to the reward of deeper connection and trust.

Things to Consider:

- For an interesting activity that facilitates codeswitching, take a look at the Personal Qualities exercise in the resource section.

- For more on what happens when extended family visits upset marital harmony, see the chapters titled Acculturation and Ethnocentrism.

PART TWO

WHAT WILL IT TAKE TO MAKE IT?

Sophie and Juan Jesus

Sophie: My goal after earning my teaching degree was to work internationally. Never in my wildest dreams did I think I would end up in rural North Carolina. The students at the high school where I work are mainly kids of settled migrant workers. Since I speak Spanish I guess that made me a good fit. The perk at this job was if I worked in an underserved community for two years, my student loans would be forgiven.

After a month I began to wonder what I had gotten myself into. The student population was tough. Education wasn't a priority, and there were teen pregnancy and gang-related problems. The teachers and staff were settled down with families. I was the only unmarried staff person, and I was really lonely.

I met Juan at the Saturday farmers market. He was taking orders from the window of El Camion Rico, a taco stand, flirting with ladies eight to eighty. I loved watching him. As we spoke we discovered we were both University of North Carolina alums. That was our beginning.

Juan: One advantage to owning a mobile restaurant is the view looking over the crowd. I noticed Sophie wandering around the market and thought she was gorgeous. We connected right away.

Sophie was different. I was intrigued by her. She'd lived in so many places and yet she felt out of place in our rural community.

I understood Sophie's loneliness. I knew what it was like to be the outsider. It happened to me when I was one of the few Latinos at the University of North Carolina and afterward when I worked in Charlotte. Before Sophie I'd dated other Anglo girls, but those relationships never lasted. I felt as if I was a cultural exchange experience for them. They never brought me around to meet their families.

With Sophie I didn't need to explain what it had been like living in two worlds. She got it. We had our fun with it too. When we ran into my friends, they took one look at Sophie and assumed I was trying to impress an Anglo. They'd make remarks in Spanish meant only for me. Sophie nailed them using humor and her perfect Spanish. Her straightforward style is one of the reasons I fell in love with her.

Shades of Bicultural

Sophie: Some people call me a Third Culture Kid (TCK) and others say Global Nomad. My parents work for the US Agency for International Development (USAID). Although I'm American, people can't quite place me ethnically, and that's fine with me. My mom is from Hawaii. She is English, Chinese and Hawaiian. My dad says his people are of Norwegian heritage with some Blackfoot Indian. In spite of how mixed their heritages are, my parents have US identities. I don't.

I grew up in four countries and now my parents live in a fifth. When I was eight we left Montana and moved to Bolivia, then Paraguay. I finished my last two years of high school in Egypt. Now my parents are in Peru. I went to international schools with kids from all over the world. The international schools had local kids, too, the country's elite. On home leave in Montana we were middle class, but overseas the government paid our tuition so we mingled with the wealthy.

TCKs like me usually fit in everywhere and feel like we belong nowhere. We are the world's greatest adjusters. I can get along with anybody, but open my heart to few. Growing up I got hurt getting close to friends who were always moving. Eventually I found it safer to stay at the superficial level. You can still have a lot of fun that way. Falling in love with Juan rocked my world. I have never trusted anyone so thoroughly.

Until I met Juan my life plan was all about adventure and living in the moment. In theory I want roots and envy Juan for having them. At the same time I am drawn toward novelty.

When Juan and I started talking about marriage, I was happy but also scared. Being with Juan taught me I could trust a man with my mixed-up cultural identity.

Last summer I took Juan to visit my parents. We joined a project working with farmers, attended embassy cocktail parties, and traveled to La Paz, Bolivia, a city I love. We danced and ate like kings. I love Juan for his curiosity; he wanted to hear my stories and see where I'd lived. Juan witnessed my wanderlust and got a taste of the travel bug too.

Juan: My parents were Mexican migrant farm workers as teenagers. They settled near Winston-Salem, North Carolina, and were US citizens by the time I was born. While I was growing up, my parents sponsored other family members from Mexico. At last count we have twenty-three relatives within five miles of my parents' house.

My parents worked long hours, intent on making a good life for us. We toed the line all week until Saturday night, when we let go and partied. I am my family's first college graduate, which means I've become a designated family leader.

After college I worked in Charlotte and moved up fast in marketing. I was proud I could send good money home. My parents thought I was crazy when I announced I was quitting to start my own mobile restaurant business. They saw my dream as a step back for the family. From their point of view, stability is more important than personal satisfaction.

When I'm passionate about something, I can be convincing. I told them I got a microloan. I modernized Mama's and Tia Anita's recipes using organic ingredients. For a while I worked eighteen-hour days. Now El Camion Rico hires cousins who need a job. Three years into it and we have a new commercial kitchen and two trucks. We're the go-to business for catering parties and weddings.

My family took to Sophie even though she is an Anglo. She listens to Mama's family stories and attends Mass on holidays. She teases my brothers on politics just to remind them she isn't going to let the men in the family think they are in charge. On the other hand, she's super respectful with the elders.

Sophie and I want to get married when her school year is finished. After traveling last summer, Sophie is pushing for us to find jobs in Latin America where I can use my business experience. It's tempting, but with my family obligations I don't know how I can leave.

The Counselors' Perspective

Like many twenty-first century couples, Juan Jesus and Sophie find comfort being with a partner who can relate to living in multi-cultural worlds while never fitting perfectly in any one of them. Although Sophie's fear of commitment as a Third Culture Kid or Global Nomad is obvious and easier to tease out, Juan's experi-ence as a second-generation immigrant presents a more subtle, personal dilemma of balancing assimilation and family loyalty.

Juan was raised with the collectivist value of putting family first. As the successful son returning home, he brought high expectations for leadership. Juan stepped up to his role. Having lived at UNC and in urban Charlotte for eight years in the mainstream culture, Juan now embraces many characteristics of individualism. Out of loyalty and respect Juan minimizes his changes when he is with family, and that is beginning to cause conflict as he and Sophie plan a life together.

Sophie's family lifestyle was one of variety, adventure, and indepen-dence with little stability outside the immediate family. Although they lived more years in collectivist cultures than individualist, the family's individualist values were supported. As US citizens they could rely on trusted homeland institutions that would provide education, health care, and other services not ordinarily available in the collectivist cultures in which they lived and worked.

Juan and Sophie are brilliant codeswitchers who thought they embraced both languages and cultures evenly. But notice in their introductions: Sophie talks about herself first and Juan talks about family first. This indicates that they have philosophical prefer-ences they may not be aware of. Most multicultural people have a first-culture world view, the one they were born into, which operates as their default world view when under stress. It is important to examine your default world views nonjudgmentally.

It helps resolve conflict when couples acknowledge their cultural preferences and get strategic about choices going forward. What form will Juan's cultural family loyalty take with Sophie? Can he risk talking with his family more openly about who he has become since he left home at age eighteen? For most bicultural people, rigid loyalty leads to resentment and eventually damages relationships. Like most people Juan has to find his own path of compromise. Denial always backfires.

Because she understands his culture, Sophie can act as a sounding board as they sort things through. How much family disappointment can Juan live with? Could Juan trust another family member to run the business? If they leave the United States, do Juan and Sophie plan to send money to the family like Juan did when he lived in Charlotte? How will that affect their work, travel, and adventure priorities?

In turn, Sophie needs to acknowledge her distrust of roots for what it is: fear of losing people and places she loves. In the past she lived by the code *it's less painful to leave before someone leaves you*, but that lack of vulnerability won't work in a committed relationship. Sophie needs a strategy for taking risks, opening up to Juan when something makes her anxious rather than clamming up and pretending everything is fine.

Right now Juan is making good money, using it to grow his business and sharing it with his family. Sophie doesn't worry about money because she comes from an educated middle-class family with a history of good employment and plenty of opportunities. She has faith in what she can achieve and is not concerned about the appearances of wealth. Juan's family is upwardly mobile in a culture where appearances of wealth are important displays of achievement for the family and in their community.

Juan and Sophie will need to keep talking about how to balance their couple life priorities while honoring some of Juan's family obligations. Sophie will need to find creative ways to honor her desire for novelty and adventure while embracing stability. There are many challenges and much work ahead. The good news is they are young, flexible, energetic, and in love.

What Has Helped

Sophie: Juan and I decided to talk to a counselor to help us through our issues about family expectations versus personal freedom. At the suggestion of the counselor we each did a Life Balance Inventory to look at how we balance our priorities. It was a good place to start.

I got in touch with the fact that my wanderlust is a normal response to my family moving every few years. It helped me modify my romance with novel experiences. The counseling also helped me appreciate that through all our family mobility, my parents modeled a strong partnership of trust and respect. I have to trust Juan's honest love. I know he is a good man. When it comes to loyalty, he is the gold standard. Now when I get uptight, I remind myself there is no reason to assume people I care about will leave just because I had so much of that growing up.

Juan: I love Sophie. I also love my family, and being an entrepreneur. My life was all out of balance with work and family until Sophie and I got serious. Now I have seen other possibilities, but with the way I was raised it's hard to break from tradition and family first. I want to try working overseas but I've got to figure out how to give back after all the sacrifices my family made for me. The task is making it all work.

Counseling gave me some insight and relief from guilt. I see how second-generation Americans are caught between traditional loyalty and being your own person.

Sophie and I have been talking about compromises that won't hurt my family overmuch. We have decided if Sophie teaches one more year and I coach a couple of my cousins to manage the business, I can afford to take a sabbatical and we can try living overseas. Truth is, my family won't like that. I don't think the way they do anymore. That's hard.

We are committed to keeping the conversation on our differences moving. We constantly talk about where to live and how to finance travel. When we have kids I want to settle close enough to see my family regularly. Sophie still struggles with the idea of one place called home. The difference is now we feel more confident we can find compromises that work for us.

Things to Consider:

- Is one or are both of you bilingual or is one of you a Third Culture Kid? How has that affected your communication?

- How does codeswitching happen in your relationship? Does it help you feel better understood? For more on this subject, see the chapter titled Codeswitching.

- If your relationship is less than a couple of years old or if you are entering a new stage of life together, consider completing the Life Balance Inventory in the resource section.

HOW CAN WE GET OUR
FAMILIES BACK?

Yitzhak and Lara

Yitzhak: As an engineering student and immigrant, I was focused on getting through my academic program when I met Lara. We met in a course in East-West theology that I took out of curiosity, but mostly because it fit my schedule. I thought it would be an easy A and was surprised by the challenging material.

Lara was a fiery class standout. She would trip up my assumptions with logic and humor. For someone so young and, from my perspective, sheltered, her insight startled me.

After that class we kept running into each other on campus and at a nearby café. We started sharing a table and eventually our life stories. Lara's enthusiasm was uplifting and her humor was outrageous, making me laugh until I was clutching my belly. By the end of the school year we were a couple.

Lara: Junior year I had to get off the fence and declare my major. My parents, who were funding my university degree, assumed I would become an accountant like my father. For them the purpose of a university education is to earn a good living and make the family proud. So I double majored: accounting for them and religious studies for me. And I did it in four years to prove I could.

Looking back, I remember Yitzhak in class lounging in the back row. I thought he was beautiful and a little exotic with his accent. He struggled with the readings but covered it nicely by presenting provocative questions. When we started going out I discovered under his bravado he is thoughtful and sensitive. Once we got to know each other we could talk freely about anything despite our backgrounds.

Ethnicity Matters

Yitzhak: After my three-year compulsory military service in Israel I was exhausted. My parents wanted me to take a break—relax, backpack in Europe or South America like many young people do. But I wanted to study engineering, and I wanted to do it in the United States. When I was sixteen I'd spent a wonderful summer living with my mother's sister, Rebecca, and her American family. I'd kept in touch and knew they would welcome me again.

I come from a lineage of proud Israeli survivors. My grandmother, Bubbeh Lena, was born in Holland and spent three years hiding during World War II in a girls' convent school. One of my grandfathers died fighting in the 1967 Arab-Israeli war. Bubbeh Lena told me she lost Rebecca to America and didn't want her oldest grandson moving there too. That didn't stop me, though. Aunt Rebecca and Uncle Irv welcomed me to their home near Detroit. I enrolled in community college until I was admitted to the University of Michigan.

I learned more about Judaism in my year with Rebecca and Irv than I had in my twenty-two years in Israel. It was strange seeing my aunt so religious when the rest of my family is so secular. When I asked my mother, she said she believed Rebecca felt guilty about leaving Israel and turned to religion for comfort.

Once I left Rebecca and Irv's home, I rarely visited for Shabbat. They sent me names of "nice" Jewish girls and were disappointed when I didn't follow up. In our senior year I invited Lara to my cousin's bar mitzvah. I remember we were nervous. At the party everyone assumed Lara was Jewish. (From Rebecca and Irv's point of view, there is no other kind of girlfriend.) When it came out Lara was Christian Chaldean, nobody was happy. By the end of the evening my relatives' warmth had turned chilly.

Lara: My parents are the children of Iraqi immigrants. Chaldeans are a proud Iraqi Christian minority who spoke the Aramaic of Jesus. After World War II Iraq enforced the Arabic language and other sanctions against us. As a result most Chaldeans no longer speak our native tongue, and many have immigrated to North America. We have a huge cultural presence in Detroit.

I remember as a child my siblings and I could walk to both sets of our grandparents' houses. I grew up spending as much time at my aunts' houses as my own. Our cousins were our best friends.

In high school we moved. We were still near our Chaldean community but no longer in its nucleus. I entered a new world that changed me forever. I was in classes with kids from different religions and ethnicities. I loved it.

My parents' expectations drove me nuts. I was supposed to excel academically and, after university, return to live at home until I married. With family I continued to be the proper daughter, but inside I knew their disappointment was inevitable. After graduation I hoped to work for an interfaith organization in Washington, DC.

When Yitzhak and I got serious I told my family I had an Israeli boyfriend. Chaldean Americans don't consider themselves Arabs, and my family isn't anti-Semitic. Still, they weren't overjoyed. When Yitzhak came for Christmas he attended our church. My parents were hospitable but they asked lots of questions about his plans to return to Israel. I think they assumed our relationship would end at graduation.

Can Love Conquer All?

Lara: For graduation my family drove up from Detroit. Yitzhak's parents flew in from Israel. We planned to announce our engagement at a picnic, but we kept it a secret when the atmosphere got tense. In hindsight we should have predicted resistance. We had become used to the open-minded university town, where multiethnic relationships are normal.

Yitzhak and I talked and stressed all night about our families. We loved them yet weren't willing to give up on our relationship to please them. Our decision to elope was impulsive and I don't regret it. We got married in the campus interfaith chapel with a few good friends in attendance. We decided to travel to Tel Aviv before moving to Kansas City, where Yitzhak had a job beginning in September.

I called my parents and told them the news. My father was furious and my mother cried. My parents liked Yitzhak, but they hadn't expected an Israeli son-in-law. Even so, I thought my family would overcome the shock of our eloping by the time we returned. I've always been the family optimist.

Yitzhak: Our first week of marriage suffered some rude awakenings. I called my parents. They were shocked and upset. We would talk about it when we visited. When I rang Aunt Rebecca and Uncle Irv to announce our marriage, they hung up on me. Such an extreme reaction made me angry and very sad. How could the warmth they had shown disappear like that?

I was grateful Lara was excited to see my country. We backpacked at Ein Gedi Beach on the Dead Sea, my favorite childhood vacation spot. We went to Jerusalem, a spiritual highlight for Lara. Our last stop was the suburbs of Tel Aviv and my family.

I hoped my parents would get over the double disappointment of my marriage to a Christian and decision to stay in the United States. I was especially worried about Bubbeh Lena, who had always been my champion. When we showed up at her house, she slammed the door. (Thankfully she opened it again.) She said she'd sit shiva if she were religious, but her manner let me know we'd get through her armor. My sisters warmed to Lara, but my parents froze us out.

We've been in Kansas City a year now and we are happy. We have good jobs and have found some friends. We are making our own way together, but we miss our families and worry over the strained relationships.

The Counselors' Perspective

As a couple Yitzhak and Lara have some family dynamics in common because they both come from collectivist clans and were raised on their families' immigration stories. They also have a common experience as third-generation immigrants, two generations removed from the immigration experience of their grandparents.

Although Yitzhak is both a third-generation and a first-generation immigrant, his experience is different than his grandparents'. He is a young man with resources and family. He can't relate experientially to the depth of his grandparents' struggle or his parents' identity conflict as second-generation immigrants. Lara has a different take on being a third-generation immigrant. She is comfortable in the country culture in which she lives. It took her intercultural marriage to make Lara aware of the older generations' resistance to living outside traditional expectations.

For Yitzhak's and Lara's grandparents (first-generation immigrants) and parents (second-generation immigrants), culture loss is a powerful force. In this case it has shown up as a sense of betrayal when Yitzhak and Lara married and planned their life. They see Yitzhak and Lara as turning their backs on sacred social and ethnic values. Similar couples need to prepare themselves to be misunderstood.

Couples rejected by families need to step away from the family attacks rather than become defensive and reactionary. For Yitzhak and Lara, living in another state produced anxiety, yet it allowed perspective. Meantime, they sent cards and e-mails. It helped them to target open-minded family members. Another bridging strategy was soliciting family stories and traditions so family members felt validated.

If the stress of family rejection happens to you, the commitment to stay empathetic and patient with each other will make a big difference. There are unknowns and surprises about the time and depth of a family rift. Not all of them have to be negative. Finding your own circle of friends and community will help you focus on your couple identity going forward, and allow you to take some joy in who you are together. If family conflict gets uncomfortably emotional, it is a good idea to get objective consultation or counseling to develop strategies that work best for your relationship and extended family dynamics.

What Has Helped

Lara: Although it was hard for us to have our families so angry with us, it has been a blessing we've had this year in Kansas City by ourselves. We needed time alone to figure out how we wanted to be as a couple. While we were at university we were students in love and didn't really think much about how to blend our cultures until we got our own apartment. For example, at home we have been cooking, eating, and dancing to Chaldean and Jewish music in addition to the other American things we both like.

We've experienced religious difference more as a philosophical conversation than as a problem. I am always taken aback when people who hear our story assume religion is the big issue. Since high school I have been a very liberal Catholic. Yitzhak is spiritual but not religious. When the time comes, we feel we will be able to find a way to raise children with a strong spiritual life. I know it won't be smooth or easy, but as I have said before, I am an optimist. And I don't give up easily.

Kansas City is a friendly city, even though there isn't the kind of diversity we are accustomed to in a big campus town like Ann Arbor. We use our humor to cope with the reality that we look like "what are you" outsiders. Sometimes after a trip to the mall, we come home and laugh hysterically about how Yitzhak, with his dark blond hair and green eyes, could pass for a Midwesterner if he didn't open his mouth, but I, the US citizen who looks Middle Eastern, get some skeptical glances. To carry on with our theme, Yitzhak is perfecting a Kansas accent and I am considering dressing conservatively and wearing Middle Eastern style makeup when we go out just to see if I get a reaction. We have found we can have fun while getting thicker skins.

We have been missing our families. In Chaldean culture, extended family relationships are everything, and now we were being treated as outsiders. I was so frustrated and hurt when Christmas came and my family didn't invite us to the family party. We drove up to Detroit anyway and stopped by with gifts. They didn't turn us away but it was tense. That hurt.

I am working on my family a little bit at a time. My two sisters are coming to visit, and that's progress. Sometimes I have a mini breakdown that we will never get back into the family circle. Other times I have a lot of hope because some family relationships are much better compared to this time last year.

Yitzhak: Although Lara and I originally wanted a big wedding, or maybe two weddings, one in each country, I think it would have been a disaster. At the picnic it was obvious our families were not ready to accept us, and we weren't willing to wait years negotiating peace with them.

We took a break to work on ourselves, and now we are working on mending relationships bit by bit. I'm talking with Bubbeh Lena on Skype, getting the stories about Holland and the early days in Israel I never heard as a child. Once in a while I slip in something I have learned about Chaldeans. My parents are still resentful I'm not coming back to Israel. They still blame Lara for my decision, but they are beginning to see how much I love her. And I know my mom wants a relationship with her future grandchildren. It's hard to be patient, but we're making progress.

My heartbreak is Aunt Rebecca and Uncle Irv. They have meant so much to me and they are my only family in the States. They are both still so angry. We don't talk and we aren't invited to visit, but I send e-mail updates and cards.

Lara and I vent to each other about our family rejections, but we know it doesn't help anything to express our anger toward them. We are spending our energy making our life together and supporting each other's long-term strategies instead. We know some family members may never accept us. We will have to live with that, and live our best life together.

Things to Consider

- Have you experienced criticism for dating or marrying outside your culture or religion? Where do you think family fear of culture and identity loss might fit into this? You might want to use Your Cultural Heritage in the resource section as a conversation starter.

- Patience and timely reaching out to family members who are critical or have cut you off is worth the effort. Sometimes elders soften with age or the birth of a baby. Consider constructing a strategy to support each other through conflict in family relationships that seems hopeless right now.

WHERE WILL WE RAISE
OUR CHILDREN?

Angie and Francois

Francois: Eight years ago I was feeling homesick and a little guilty about taking a research position in Minneapolis rather than returning to Haiti. I had already been away six years for medical training and was anxious to go home and begin practicing medicine. However, I couldn't pass up an opportunity to join the hospital's research team.

I met Angie at the hospital staff open house. She was pretty and easygoing, but what really drew me to her was her sharp wit. She seemed genuinely interested in my dream to build a pediatric clinic with public health outreach in Haiti. That first night we met she challenged me, saying I should include parent education and mental health screening. I was intrigued by her ideas and assertive enthusiasm. Then she offered to show me around Minneapolis. Before long we were spending our weekends together.

Angie: I was immediately drawn to Francois. His energy was infectious. He didn't look or walk or talk like a local. He had unique mannerisms and his skin was darker than that of other African Americans I knew. I couldn't place his accent. His passion impressed me. I had five years' experience as a hospital social worker and was beginning to lose faith until Francois's vision for public health in Haiti carried me back to a hopeful place.

Francois loved pediatrics, but he wasn't obsessed with work. We started hanging out, hiking in the countryside, and exploring the nightlife. Even though Francois had a brutal schedule with medicine and research, he knew how to laugh and keep his spirits up under just about any circumstances. He seemed to have it all balanced. I couldn't help falling in love.

Family Matters

Francois: I was shocked my parents reacted so coldly when I called to tell them I had asked Angie to marry me. The timing was perfect. Angie and I had been together a year, my research grant would end soon, and Angie was excited about moving to Haiti to work with families and children.

I had been telling my parents how smart, talented, and beautiful Angie was for months, but somehow they didn't want to believe we were serious. Although they never said anything, I knew my parents hoped that after my training I would marry a Haitian woman, preferably from our social circle. They were not enthusiastic about a "foreigner" in the family, even though our family had lived in France for eight years.

All my life, my parents had stressed how our family has been prominent in Haiti since the slave rebellion in 1791 that led to Haitian independence. Expectations go with that legacy. My parents didn't think an American would fit in or understand us.

Angie: The first time I brought Francois home to Chicago was for Thanksgiving. We'd only been dating a few months. My parents were, as usual, warm and welcoming. My dad is retired army and works as a high school history teacher. My mom owns a business specializing in financial planning for African American women.

My parents grew up on the south side of Chicago in a poor neighborhood with limited opportunities. They were high school sweethearts who did well in school but couldn't afford college. The army offered a way out and up, and for my parents it worked. My dad became a respected noncommissioned officer, and both my parents finished college as the army moved us around the country. They raised my brother and me to work hard and give back to those less fortunate. It's no surprise I'm a social worker.

Like most military families, we are a tight family. As Francois and I got serious, I shared my feelings for him with my mom, but she was not thrilled. She was worried that he was too foreign looking and elite acting. She was concerned he came from a chauvinistic culture. My parents were skeptical that we'd make it with all our differences, and they definitely didn't want me to move to Haiti. But eventually they put their feelings aside, gave me a very special wedding, and welcomed Francois into the family.

Our Dream and Our Reality

Angie: We moved to Haiti when I was four months pregnant with Annie. Everything was great at first. I took six months off after she was born, and then I wanted to be at the clinic three days a week. Francois was surprised but OK with it. Francois's parents were thrilled with their new grandbaby, but when they found out I planned to return to work alongside Francois they pitched a fit. "What will people think of Angie working at the clinic with a baby at home? She should be entertaining and thinking about your career."

67

The clinic was tough. Although I tried hard, the language barrier made it difficult for patients to trust me. My career has been working with the underserved, but in Haiti I couldn't connect. It broke my heart. It was humiliating. I became depressed and asked Francois to find a position back in the United States. Francois's parents were furious at me, but they never said a word directly. In Haiti I felt unwanted everywhere.

Francois: In Haiti we have significant language and social class barriers. In a strange way, it's comforting because it's tradition and people know how to live with it. Our system is changing slowly, but you can't rush change, especially in Haiti. As a people we ease into change, avoid conflict, and maintain relationships that bring long-term outcomes.

I think Angie expected too much of herself too quickly. She has a strong personality and is very American. She wanted parents at the clinic to make changes they weren't ready for. The poverty, domestic violence, and lack of protection for women really upset her. The patients could tell and they would avoid her.

People in my family's circle welcomed Angie even though they thought her very odd for wanting to work at the clinic after Annie was born. Her behavior was confusing to everyone, regardless of social status.

By the time Annie was three, Angie was pregnant again. We argued about staying in Haiti versus an offer I had to return to the research project in Minneapolis. I love Angie. I was worried about her and I wanted the second pregnancy to go well. Though it wrenched my heart, I took the job in Minneapolis. I think we both knew that moving to Minneapolis was only a temporary solution.

Who Do We Want to Be?

Francois: Our departure from Haiti was painful. My parents blamed Angie for their disappointment. I was torn. We all cried. I wanted to stay in Haiti but not at the cost of my wife and children. I will always ache for my Haitian roots: the flowers from our garden, the street music, Haitian food, and the benefit of having a supportive, well-connected family.

I feel secure when I am with my extended family. Here in America no one is available to help. I am Haitian, not African American. If I stay in the United States, what will be my children's cultural identity? What will be our family identity? Will my family and my traditions be lost if I stay in America? What about my dream for public health in Haiti?

Angie: I have always been flexible and open-minded. Usually I love a challenge. I was the school-aged kid who led teams and earned citizenship awards. So naturally I was shocked when I found I didn't get along with most Haitians unless I did it 100 percent their way. Tradition rules in Haiti. I didn't have much wiggle room, and that rigidity doesn't fit for me. I got depressed and didn't recognize myself.

My father-in-law, as head of the household, makes the important decisions, and my mother-in-law defers to him even though she has day-to-day influence over the household. I found the subtle use of women's power manipulative and was even more shocked when it worked. It really scared me that my mother's fears about women's roles in Haitian society were spot on.

Francois is not as domineering as his father, but I was taken aback when he slipped into Haitian cultural attitudes the longer we

69

were there. I love him, but I was afraid of losing myself. I talked to friends and my parents for support. My mom kept saying, "Just come home. How can you raise your children there?"

The Counselors' Perspective

Angie and Francois are bonded by their idealism, both in their relationship and in their devotion to service for others. They were both disturbed by Angie's culture shock. She had moved several times regionally in the United States and hadn't thought it would be difficult to move internationally. Francois was confused because he had adjusted easily to the United States. It rocked their relationship until they started examining why Angie's culture shock was so powerful.

Angie grew up in a mobile, career military family based on American individualist values. Her parents raised their children to have a sense of personal autonomy and to trust that outside institutions, like schools and government, can and do work well and help people. Angie and her brother reaped the benefits of the hard-won civil and individual rights battles of her parents' generation. As an adult, Angie is successful at making creative decisions, facilitating fair treatment, and empowering her patients to self-advocate.

Francois's family has classic collectivist cultural values. Everyone in Francois's family and community has a role that makes for a secure sense of belonging. Family reputation is essential. Francois's family gets things done by relying on trusted, generations-long relationships without which few important social transactions or job advancements would be possible.

In-law meddling in a couple's relationship is even more challenging when one family is collectivist and the other individualist. Angie and Francois are talking about deeply grounded philosophical world view conflicts in addition to the usual relationship conflicts, such as how to negotiate a budget and what to eat for dinner. Angie and Francois need to listen carefully to each other's most cherished memories, traditions, and beliefs. Their challenge as a couple is to negotiate and combine, choose, define, and create shared beliefs, and then decide how to describe their decisions to both extended families.

Even the most loving, open-minded families assume their children will follow their cultural beliefs, language, and traditions. For Francois's collectivist family, breaking with tradition is more devastating than for Angie's individualist family, who are accustomed to their children thinking more independently.

When grandchildren arrive, the emotional expectations of both sides of the family escalate. Both sets of grandparents want to see their family's traditions take precedence, and when they don't they feel threatened. They use the weapons they know best: loyalty and guilt.

Francois and Angie are in a major life stage transition, making decisions on where and how to raise their children. They will need to have an open-ended conversation on gender roles and parenting philosophies in order to negotiate how to model values for their children. It will also be helpful for them to strategize around living in the United States and visiting Haiti without being defensive.

The goal for both is to feel free and flexible to fit more comfortably in both cultures. They know another move is coming, and they have to be proactive about finding the right fit. But if they know they don't have to lose their identities along the way, any relocation will be more comfortable.

What Has Helped

Angie: I felt better immediately after we resettled in Minneapolis. That's when I took an honest look at myself and realized how I had misunderstood my own culture shock. I hadn't considered how different Haitian culture was from mine.

Because Francois had fit in so well in Minneapolis, I assumed it would be the same for me. I wish I had talked to people who had lived in Haiti, read books, watched movies, and asked Francois more questions before we moved.

Coming home I understood why Francois could get so sad talking about people, places, smells, and foods he missed. I could never tease him out of it when the loneliness came on. Now we talk about culture shock and cultural grieving in a completely different way. We're consciously bringing more of the Haitian experience into our lives. I'm not saying I want to grow old in Haiti, and I am not saying I want my daughter to take on the traditional woman's role in Haiti, but I am saying it took leaving Haiti and coming back to the United States to really understand another culture.

When we lived in Haiti my mom's fears about living there forever came out in angry e-mails directed toward Francois's family. The communication was so upsetting to me, I would get pounding headaches. Since returning, my parents and I have had serious conversations about living between cultures. Mom finally told me that when we lived in Haiti she felt scared I would give up my US identity. I wish we could have understood the power of family loyalty then, but I am glad we are talking about it now.

Francois: This has been a hard road. One positive is Angie truly understands the immigrant experience. But I wish I had prepared her better. Then perhaps her experience would not have been so difficult. We were idealistic and naive. It was a mistake to assume just because we love each other everything would be smooth crossing cultures.

I think it was easier for me coming to the United States as a single man in my twenties. I was studying hard among a community of people with the same goal. When there was time to relax, friends took me under their wings. By the time I met Angie, I had been in the United States six years. Being back in Haiti activated my love of my country and the importance of my family. Annie, our first child, learned Haitian French from the time she was born. Now I am speaking it with both children as a way of keeping home alive in them.

Angie and I have been looking at all the options for life and work. I have applied for a position at the Centers for Disease Control in Atlanta that will allow me to align with the clinic in Haiti and visit regularly. Angie is looking for school-based social work positions in Atlanta so she will have summers and longer school holidays that we could spend in Haiti. She has even agreed to spend holidays in Haiti even if I'm not able to be there the entire time. Nothing would make me happier than to know she really means to raise our children biculturally.

We are finding our way. It's not perfect. We are learning to check with each other, to sort out if the problem is based on cultural differences or simply the influence of a bad day. Our parents remain competitive about which traditions should have more influence on the children. But we are committed on working on who we are together, and that makes us both happy.

Things to Consider:

- Where would you place each of your families on the collectivist to individualist cultural spectrum when you were growing up? Where would you place yourselves today?

- When you plan a visit to the "other" country or culture, make a date to discuss concerns about in-law expectations. What concerns do you have that your partner will culturally align with his or her family? When you visit, take some moments every day to check in and create strategies to alert each other so you can reconnect if one of you feels isolated or left out.

- When conflict occurs in your in-law relationships, could cultural competition have a part in it? Could the grandparents fear that their grandchildren will not be at home in their culture?

HOW CAN WE RECONCILE
EAST AND WEST?

Inge and Arnulf

Arnulf: After the Berlin Wall fell in 1989, Western investment flooded the Eastern Zone to foster development and modernization. Before that I spent years working on boring engineering projects in my native Dresden. Suddenly I was working for an international engineering company, traveling to Frankfurt and Paris. It was an exciting, hopeful time. There were so many opportunities, so much energy and enthusiasm. It was something that people of my generation, born and raised in the Communist era, had not had much experience with. It was invigorating. It made me feel that anything was possible. It was at this point that Inge joined our company.

She came to us as a secretary. Inge was very young, just graduated from university, and quite beautiful. Very quickly it was discovered that her fluent English could be invaluable. I spoke some English, and until Inge came along I had acted as the English-speaking liaison whenever necessary. I was never comfortable with this and was quite relieved when Inge took these duties. We began working closely together. Her youthful enthusiasm was contagious. She grasped complex concepts quickly and was very inspiring for one so young. Inge was just a few years older than my own children, and I was hopeful that they would turn out so well. Inge and I became good friends. Originally, I had no romantic ideas about the two of us. I had been married before and had two teenagers. It was Inge who changed my attitude.

Inge: I had always thought of anyone from my parents' generation as old-fashioned. Arnulf changed that. He had adjusted to the change from communism to democracy well. He had traveled to foreign countries and was successful. Arnulf was a wonderful storyteller and we laughed a lot. I felt respect and friendship for him. Also love. If we talked of anything outside of work, he was sweet, almost shy. I knew from other secretaries that Arnulf had been divorced for years and that he was a devoted father.

At first Arnulf wanted to keep our relationship within the office and only as friends. It took a little while, but I changed his mind. It helped that his children liked me. They said that my being younger was a good thing. We had some things in common, I could give them good advice, and they knew I would not try to be a mother to them. If they had not liked me, it would have been over—that is how devoted a father Arnulf is. Our wedding was a truly joyful occasion.

Not All Change Comes Easily

Inge: The company we worked for had a branch in the United States. After our son Theo was born, Arnulf and I were given the opportunity to transfer. Arnulf was reluctant to leave his other children, but they were excited to visit us in the States. Besides, Arnulf would be traveling back to Germany quite regularly. Also, we thought it would be easier to live internationally before our son began school. If we didn't like it, we could always go back.

Arnulf: The first years in America reminded me of the first years after the Wall fell, very new and exciting. I worked hard to improve my English. Theo grew quickly and my older children visited every winter and summer. By the time Katja—she prefers to be called Katie—was born, we were comfortable in our new life. We had some friends in the local German community and Theo was in preschool. We were raising him bilingually so that he could live in both countries easily.

When it was time for Theo to start school, I wanted to return to Germany. Inge argued that the American system of education was better, and that our children would benefit from the freedoms and many choices here. I agreed, and we stayed.

Inge: Theo and Katie are typical American teenagers, even with dual citizenship. They both speak German and know their culture, but they call themselves Americans. This has caused conflict between Arnulf and me. It was easier when our children were small. Now they have minds and opinions of their own, and Arnulf doesn't understand these young people of today. He thinks they take for granted their freedoms, and he hates to see his children be so disrespectful and entitled. According to Arnulf, his older children never talked back and were always obedient. I tell him it's more difficult for our children, because there are so many choices they must make for themselves.

Arnulf and I grew up in a society where choices were made for us. Living under the Communist regime has made it hard for him to understand that struggling with making choices is a normal and healthy part of growing up. He does not see modern life as I do. We argue quite a bit about this. This leads to other disagreements as well. Before we agreed on most things; now we rarely see eye to eye.

Arnulf: I do not approve of the way my daughter dresses. She comes home from the shops with short skirts and tight blouses. Her mother says she looks lovely and so grown up. Why do young girls want to look grown up? Let them be children! Katie says this is the fashion and there are no other styles to choose from. My mother and sisters sewed clothing for themselves and created their own fashions. Katie does not sew or knit or cook. Inge learned to sew, but she did not teach Katie. I worry that Inge is encouraging our daughter to be a wild, free girl. And my son? Theo does not know what he wants to study. At his age, I knew exactly what I was going to do. He says he wants a liberal arts education before he studies something that will help him make money. I told him that I will not support him if he cannot get a job.

Inge says I am narrow-minded. I remind her that she and I both studied and worked hard all our lives. She says she wants our children to know what it is like to be young and have opportunities and experience life. I am tired of our debates. I grow tired of this society. There were some things under the Communist government that were not so bad. Of course I would never go back to that, but life was not as complicated as it is now. And young people were raised to have respect and a purpose. Also, I miss my homeland, my older children, and grandchildren. I am encouraging Theo and Katie to attend university in Germany. I have saved enough money to live comfortably. In a few years I want to retire and return to Germany to live.

Inge: My life is here. My children's lives are here. I don't want to go.

The Counselors' Perspective

Age at immigration makes a difference. In their early years together, neither Inge nor Arnulf considered their age gap to be a factor. Now the generational differences matter. Generally speaking, the younger one immigrates, the easier it is to adapt to a new culture. The older you are when you leave your home country, the more history and thus the more of yourself is left behind. This loss is important to acknowledge, honor, and address. Every person adapts in his or her own way. It is common for one member of a couple to feel more comfortable in the new culture. And when your partner adapts differently, it's easy to take that personally. Culture loss and cultural grieving take on different flavors in a couple from different generations, because cultures, even highly regimented ones, change and evolve over time.

One common misconception is that people moving from one Western society to another aren't making much of a change and that acculturation should be easy. This is not so. True, you will find Starbucks, McDonald's, and United Colors of Benetton in Los Angeles, New York, London, and Munich. But we have to look deeper than chain stores for cultural connections.

Inge grew up much more aware of what life was like in the West through music and print materials made available to her and fellow students of the English language as they prepared to represent their government's interests abroad. She was eager to experience these things for herself and was prepared to embrace all that was new. Arnulf was not exposed to Western influences until he was middle-aged. His life under the Communist government had been restricted, but it was what he had always known. He knew who he was in that society and was comfortable in that identity. After unification he was able to adapt with little conflict, because his day-to-day experiences centered on what was already familiar: work and family. Moving to the United States and parenting teenagers again stretched him far beyond his comfort zone. He felt ill equipped to deal with the new ideas, attitudes, and lifestyles. He felt alone and left behind.

What Has Helped

Inge: I became a US citizen as soon as I could. Arnulf had always said he would become a US citizen when he felt like one. Needless to say, he still has his German passport. I think we both felt hurt and betrayed by the other's decision. I wondered about Arnulf's loyalty to our family, because he kept talking about going back to Germany to be closer to the family he left behind. I wondered if he still loved me.

Arnulf: It was not easy to discuss my feelings with my wife. It was not easy identifying what I was feeling in order to talk to her about them. She couldn't understand why I missed Germany so much, and why I wanted to be near my children and grandchildren. For some reason, she saw that as proof of me being less committed to her and our children. This was not true.

Inge: Even after so many years together there were insecurities and doubts. Now I better understand the way Arnulf feels about being split in two. I don't want him to have to live that way. I don't want our family to live that way. I don't want any of us to feel we have to choose. I became aware of how much I saw our family as two families: his from before and ours now. From our courtship days I felt I was playing tug of war with his older children with Arnulf as the rope, wanting his loyalty to be with me. It took a while to see that there was no one really pulling on the other end. Arnulf has love enough for us all. We compromised and now have a vision for our future that we can both be content with.

Arnulf: I am an engineer, a problem solver. I proposed this solution: when I retire, as long as the children are in school, we will live in the United States and vacation in Germany. That way Inge can continue to work as much as she wants. When the children finish their educations, we will live for one half of the year in the United States and the other six months in Germany. Inge can retire or continue working, whatever she wishes at that point. It has taken negotiation and fine-tuning, but that remains the basic plan. It was Inge who added that if the children go to German universities or choose to live there as adults, we can spend even more time there! When she said that, I knew she truly understood how I felt about spending more time as a *whole* family.

Things to Consider:

- If there is a marked age difference between you and your partner, how does it affect your relationship?

- Talk with your partner about the eras in which you grew up. Compare your Culturegrams with this as a focus. Do the differences affect how each of you sees the world? Does this affect how you relate to your children, authority, or society in general? If so, what kinds of conversations and problem solving strategies would be useful for you to come to better understandings and to create more options?

- Do the Personal Qualities exercise in the resource section. What can you learn from and about each other?

WHAT HAPPENS WHEN
THE GOOD LIFE DISAPPEARS?

Robert and Keira

Robert: I met Keira at an Irish pub. Her crowd of girlfriends was the center of attention, singing along with the band in Gaelic. My buddy and I bought them a round of drinks and by the end of the evening I had Keira's phone number. I wondered if she would have any problems going out with a black man. She didn't.

I was traveling constantly at the time, so ours was a friendly off-and-on relationship for a couple of years, which worked well for both of us. Then we had a magical weekend getaway that changed everything. By year's end we were married.

New York City in the late 1990s was a great place to be a mixed-race couple. Our friends looked pretty much like a United Nations of black, white, and mixed ethnic couples. The economy was booming and we were having a great time. We would get stared at when we'd spend weekends in small towns or rural areas, but we blew them off and didn't get uptight about what strangers thought about us.

In fourteen years of marriage, we've been blessed. Sure, we've had the usual ups and downs between balancing children and work, but most of the time we're really good together. We're both normally even tempered, so the hostility over how to resolve our financial problems took us by surprise.

Keira: The night I met Robert I'd had a few beers and was singing with abandon, trying to forget about my last patient in the emergency room who had lost his leg in a motorcycle accident. I remember noticing Robert dressed to the nines, thinking he looked like a model from *GQ*.

I accepted his invitation to dinner because right away there was chemistry. I had a few concerns, though. I had never dated an African American and I wasn't sure what going out with him would be like. I was nervous there would be push back from friends when we went out together. I needn't have worried. After a couple of dates color disappeared and all I noticed was Robert's intelligence and generosity. We also found common interests in art, movies, and food, which deepened our connection.

I didn't want a committed relationship when I met Robert. I had erratic shifts at the hospital and Robert traveled all the time. I felt safe I could keep my promise to myself to not allow a man to become more important than my freedom. Two years later I did a one-eighty. By that time, I knew Robert was the one for me, and I still think it's true, in spite of the fact money problems are tearing us apart.

Roots and Money

Robert: In the 1930s my grandparents were part of the African American migration that left the Deep South for the West to escape the Jim Crow laws that kept them in poverty. My parents married right out of high school. My dad apprenticed and got his electrician's license while my mom worked at a Kmart. A few years later they started the first African American-owned electrical contracting business in Portland, Oregon. By the time I was in high school they were mentoring other African American-owned businesses.

Success was important to my parents, and they knew they had earned theirs. The summer before sixth grade we moved to an all-white neighborhood. My brother, sister, and I were the only African American kids at our school and we lived under a microscope. We felt that we had to excel to fit in. Our parents repeated their mantra that it was our responsibility to prove that college-bound African Americans are not just athletes.

After college I couldn't leave my hometown fast enough. I got a job with an advertising firm in Manhattan and it was a perfect fit. When I met Keira I was having the time of my life and felt there was nowhere to go but up. And until now that proved to be true.

Keira: My parents were raised in a small village in southern Ireland where both their families have lived for generations. When they immigrated they settled in a blue-collar Irish American neighborhood that kept the small-town Irish mind-set. To this day my Mom does everything without going more than six blocks from home. My siblings live nearby. My oldest brother went to work for my uncle Liam, and my next two brothers are firefighters in Boston. My twin sister got married at nineteen, but I had other ideas. My high school counselor helped me find a scholarship to nursing school. After I graduated I got a job at a hospital in New York City. My departure was a hot topic of conversation for the gossipers in our neighborhood.

Living in New York was a dream come true. I visited museums and the galleries. I got my Irish fix shopping at specialty stores or at the pub Saturday nights with friends. I was feeling very good about myself when I met Robert.

Robert and I seemed to have a charmed life until recently. In spite of our parents' early concerns about our mixed marriage, it wasn't an issue for us. We made a circle of friends we cherished, had a beautiful home in a great neighborhood, and our kids were in good schools. Robert always worked long hours and sometimes traveled, but that gave me the chance to take the kids to Boston for visits.

Robert: I managed to keep my job during my company's restructuring, and for a while I thought I might survive the layoffs. Then I got my notice with a small severance. After that life unraveled. Having to compete with twentysomethings at age fifty for short-term consulting contracts has been humiliating. For months I transferred money from our savings without telling Keira. The truth is, we didn't have much cushion even *before* I lost my job. I lived under the illusion these were my prime earning years and I had the Midas touch.

I can't stand the thought of losing our brownstone, leaving the neighborhood where I feel like we belong, and facing financial ruin in front of our friends and my family. I know I wouldn't actually do it, but there are times when I think suicide would be better for me than living in shame.

Keira: I am equal parts worried sick about Robert's depression and furious over the betrayal. Now we are close to losing our home, and we will have to take the kids out of the schools they love in the middle of the school year. I admit I have loved our lifestyle, but money and image aren't everything to me. I look at this as fate. Robert is a victim of circumstances; he is not a failure as a husband and father, but Robert doesn't see it that way. I'm not embarrassed to cut back and work full time again. We never fought about money, but now it's taken over. We are having a hard time remembering all the good things about our relationship.

The Counselors' Perspective

The subject of money is loaded with baggage from this couple's cultural heritage, family social class expectations, and current stage of life.

Couples who have "enough" money to do the things important to them, whatever that may be, often do not have deep conversations about the meaning of money. Getting clear about each partner's philosophy and values around money can be painful to bring out into the light of day. Many people intuitively know this and avoid the subject altogether, as Robert and Keira did.

Like most people, Robert's and Keira's values around money have direct ties to their families' ethnic and cultural values, and, in Robert's case, the trauma of being poor.

Although they didn't often speak about it, the family stories of Robert's grandparents' experience and the shame that accompanied it are a burden still alive in the family psyche. Robert and his siblings could feel the pressure to be successful, but didn't connect it with the family history of racism and lack of opportunity in the Deep South of the early twentieth century. They didn't connect it with the legacy that if you don't acquire wealth and power, you lose your freedom.

Robert was raised with a strong work ethic. His parents' intelligence, energy, and role modeling gave him confidence to strike out on his own, thousands of miles from home. Nonetheless, his family had not prepared him to know the difference between situational unemployment and complete failure.

Robert followed the family script of upward mobility without much insight into why he felt so driven. When Robert lost his job, shame and fear of loss of status led him to hide the crisis from Keira. His secrets led him into depression and more shame.

Going forward, it will help Robert to step back and consider how money and appearances have played a role in his life, and review his feelings of helplessness in light of generations of family trauma. If Robert and Keira can talk and stay clear that his grandparents' fear and shame do not belong to him in the twenty-first century, it will help Robert to realize he is suffering from an illogical fear. Losing money does not mean he will lose his family, friends, and face in the community forever.

In Keira's family, extra money went to Ireland or the church. Her family had pride in living simply, because everyone else they knew lived the same way. There was no shame in not having much; in fact, Keira grew up hearing her parents' suspicions about the character of people who had wealth and relished its display. Keira enjoyed the lifestyle and status she and Robert had but sometimes felt guilty. Rather than talk about her conflicting feelings about money and status, Keira shied away from thinking deeply or talking with Robert about money. Her solution was to avoid her discomfort by letting Robert handle all the finances.

Multicultural, multiethnic couples need to pay more attention to the role of money in their lives than a couple from the same ethnicity or culture. When you come from the same cultural background, there are shared traditions you both understand, and you use those values as a safety net or as a baseline to talk about touchy topics like finances. When you come from different traditions or social classes, it's a lot more work to evolve your couple philosophy and values about money. The end product will be well worth the trouble. Keeping an open conversation on money through your couple life stages will help your relationship through difficult financial choices as they emerge.

Major financial troubles are more traumatic at the stage of middle adulthood and beyond. By the midforties most couples are solidly into their careers, feeling pretty good about their contributions to the world of work, and finding ways to give back to family and community. When people get out of sync with what feels right at their life stage, it can be a huge blow to their self-esteem. What helps is staying connected, having nonjudgmental conversations, and listening carefully to each other's perspective and feelings about what's not working. Creative problem solving can help each person deal with unexpected hardships.

What Has Helped

Robert: I never thought about why appearances and having money was so important until our financial crisis. My career and lifestyle had come so easily. I worked hard and was good at my job. I was never passed over for a promotion and the bonuses came in every year. In some weird way I thought I was invulnerable.

Without thinking about it I had locked myself into a high-maintenance lifestyle. What Keira didn't know is the vacations we took and the kids' school tuition meant we hadn't been saving for years.

When I lost my job I was so ashamed about how I'd handled things. I couldn't bear to face Keira and our friends.

When I disclosed the situation with our finances, she was outraged. She was also worried about how depressed I was and insisted we see a counselor. The counselor was helpful in getting us to talk about money and shame and how to live with our mistakes.

While I was trying to figure out how to tell my extended family we would probably sell the house and transfer the kids to public school, Keira got a full-time nursing job. We've told some of our friends about what's going on, and it is a relief. It also hurts to feel so exposed. The positive outcome is that more friends and colleagues are helping with referrals for work, and things might not be as bad as I thought.

Keira: I was angry with Robert for the mess we're in, but the counselor helped me see he didn't make this problem all by himself. We've always talked about everything except finances. I loved our lifestyle and the ability to give our kids wonderful experiences I never envisioned as a child. Looking back I can see how Robert tried to include me in financial decisions, but I avoided getting involved because I felt guilty about how much everything was costing and I didn't want to deal with it. My family culture has a love-hate relationship with money. It's been a painful lesson but I've learned I can't hide from what is uncomfortable.

Robert and I have been seeing a financial counselor, and that helped us put a realistic plan in place. We might be able to keep the house. The other good news is we're getting back to the common values we share. We have hope that in the future we'll talk openly about our money and what we want to do with it as a couple.

Things to Consider:

- Have you and your partner had conversations about the way your family culture or ethnicity has influenced your relationship with money?

- Families that have known ethnic or class prejudice can be very sensitive about appearances and status. Do you have a family legacy around responsibility to stay on an upwardly mobile path? If so, what are the consequences if you don't conform?

WHO IS THE MAN IN
THE MIRROR?

Brian and Melinda

Brian: I think when people first meet Melinda and me, they're struck by the way we complement each other. Let me tell you, it was like that from the start. We just clicked. I don't know how; I don't know why; I just know I'm the luckiest guy on earth because of it!

Melinda: For the most part, I agree with what Brian just said, although I have some ideas as to how and why. And let me add, I'm pretty lucky, too. Don't get us wrong, though—we've been together for sixteen years, and we've worked hard on our relationship every day for every one of those years. So call us lucky *and* relentless!

Brian: Yeah, Melinda probably had it harder than I did at the beginning. My friends thought I struck gold when I first introduced Melinda to them. I mean, she had—and still has—it all, personality, looks, and brains. They looked from me to her to me to her, and didn't know what to say. It was funny. Then later when I was alone with my friends, they teased me with stuff like: "How much did you pay her to go out with you?" and "She must've lost a bet." They couldn't believe she'd be into a guy like me. With that gorgeous blue-eyed brunette on my arm, they thought—and I knew—I had it made.

Melinda: I admit that was a little hard. People stared. Brian thought it was funny. I didn't. But frankly, when I was with him, the looks were easy to ignore. My friends and family had questions, too. They didn't think he was quite my type. My boyfriends up until then had all been stereotypical corn-fed all-American boys. Now here I was becoming serious about this funny, skinny Asian guy, with an even funnier accent, who's younger and shorter than me. What was I thinking?

Brian: Let me tell you about my accent. It's honest. You see, I was adopted from Korea when I was seven months old. I grew up outside of Memphis, Tennessee, with my parents—they're both white; my younger sister, Cheryl, also adopted from Korea, but we're not blood relations; and our youngest sister, Vicky, who is our parents' biological child. I never caught flack about my accent until I went to college. Folks in Arizona looked twice when they heard my Southern drawl. There was a definite disconnect. I decided it would be smart to lose the accent fast. The drawl comes back when I'm with family and friends or when I'm tired. Sometimes if people ask me to, I lay it on thick to get a good laugh.

Melinda: He calls it his party trick. One day our son John came home from kindergarten mad as could be. When we asked what happened, John said his friend had laughed about his daddy's funny accent. John told us he punched his friend in the arm and said: "My daddy doesn't have an accent! And it's not funny!" Then he asked us: "What's an accent?"

Brian: Poor kid. He didn't know what he was defending. Now we make a point of laughing about how, after a visit to Tennessee, we all talk with a Southern drawl.

The Rub

Melinda: That's our issue. Our family is one big mishmash. To outsiders, Brian and I look like we shouldn't go together. Our kids look like both of us, and at the same time, they don't really look like either of us. It wasn't so noticeable until we started traveling for vacations and we got what we call "The Look." There are lots of multiracial families in our area, so being stared at was new to the kids. When the kids and I commented on people's double takes, Brian had three responses: he didn't notice anything, said we were imagining things, or suggested we just ignore it. I figured that growing up in a multiracial family would have given him insights and tools he could pass on to our kids. They sure needed it, and I couldn't really help them. Brian's responses were not helpful.

Brian: Melinda grew up in a typical all-American household: Mom, Dad, two kids, a dog, two-car garage.

Melinda: That's right. I'm from Ohio. Growing up, everyone I knew was pretty much like everyone else. No one stood out and people liked it that way. When I brought Brian home it was a big deal. In my family, if you bring someone home and it's not the holidays, it's because that person's going to start calling Mom and Dad "Mom" and "Dad." And that's where we were. We came home to announce our engagement. My family was great. But other people were skeptical. I didn't know what to make of this weirdness I was seeing in people I'd known all my life. I looked to Brian to help me understand, but he didn't see a need. First I was disappointed in them, and then I got mad at Brian. I felt that by not responding, he was giving them permission to continue being rude.

Brian: Nothing had prepared Melinda for being an outsider. From the start she expected me to help her. The problem was I didn't know what to do either. My family is known and respected in our hometown, so there were no hassles growing up. But when we visited Melinda's parents, people looked at us like we were from another planet. One time an elderly gentleman approached me in a store, said he'd served in Okinawa, and started speaking Japanese. I answered in English and he looked surprised. He asked where I'm from and looked confused when I told him Tennessee. Then he said, "No, son. Where are you *from?*"

Melinda: This whole issue actually caused a lot of friction between Brian and me, and it got worse when it affected the kids. I thought maybe Brian and I had some culture clash issues. His response was, "Culture clash? What culture clash? We're both Americans, honey." Like I said, not helpful. Eventually it occurred to me that although Brian's parents are wonderful, loving people, they didn't help Brian and Cheryl get in touch with their Korean roots at all. I really wanted Brian to take his heritage more seriously so he could help our children deal better with the outside world. He kept laughing it off, and I got angry and resentful.

Brian: I didn't get where Melinda was coming from. It felt like she wanted me to be someone I wasn't. I tried to explain to her that I'm not Korean. I may look it, but that's not how I feel, and she accused me of denying my true feelings. Frankly, I never really thought about being Korean. Being Southern was a bigger deal to me than being a Korean adoptee.

The Counselors' Perspective

Adoptees and other ethnic minorities raised in the majority culture will often say they feel "white." There are also many people who identify as minorities who are not identified as such by the larger community because they don't look it. Having your feet in two or more cultures is a delicate balancing act. It requires self-awareness and solid codeswitching abilities.

In Brian's case, his upbringing didn't require him to develop either. Later experiences, including those as a university student, helped him hone social survival skills. He learned to use his Southern accent to his advantage by turning it into a "party trick." In this way, he could turn it on or off, and no one could use it against him.

Having children is often a catalyst to go on a deeper search for identity. For people like Brian who feel they belong within a certain group yet the outside world doesn't acknowledge their membership, the rejection can be a shock to the system. In order to help children answer age-old questions like "Who am I?" and "Where do I belong?" it is necessary for adults to honestly address these questions themselves. Brian and Melinda grew up in relatively sheltered, close-knit communities; therefore, raising multiethnic children in a large city posed certain challenges. As the ethnic minority member of the couple, it fell to Brian to pave the way for the rest of his family. As an adoptee who had spent a lot of energy avoiding those universal questions, Brian was not only frustrated but also afraid of the responsibility.

What Has Helped

Melinda: It took a jolt for me to understand Brian's point of view. One day I asked him what he saw when he looked in the mirror. He said, and I quote, "A white man." That was a shock. I mean, here's this beautiful Asian man seeing himself as someone totally different from what the rest of the world sees. His answer told me I had a lot to work on. To be honest, part of what first drew me to him was his Asian appearance. I thought he was incredibly attractive. Then as we got to know each other, I just saw him for him, not his ethnicity. But if someone brought it up, I'd identify him as being Korean American. I'd never considered him white, yet that's how he sees himself.

Looking back, I can see how he used his wonderful sense of humor to deflect people's comments about the disconnect between his appearance and his—well, his true being. Avoiding the issue with other people helped him avoid it himself. What has helped? Teamwork. I learned that it wasn't just his job to figure this out. We had to do it together.

Brian: Melinda calls me on my bullshit. I had a lot of work to do, too, and it wasn't easy. I took a hard, honest look at how I see myself and how I relate to the outside world. I'd never talked with either of my sisters about what it was like for them growing up in our family, so I brought it up. They were resistant at first, but they gradually got into it.

At a recent family holiday celebration, my kids noticed how Cheryl and I stood out against the rest of our white family. Then they figured out that they did, too. It was also the first time Vicky told us how hard it was for her to grow up with two older siblings who looked nothing like her. She remembered feeling like the odd kid out. She thought that our parents loved Cheryl and me more than her. We were the kids they chose; she was the kid they got stuck with. Cheryl and I remember thinking that our parents loved her more than us. She was the kid they'd always wanted; we were the ones they took because they couldn't have their own. That got us to comparing memories. It was striking how we each remembered the same events in different ways.

My sisters told me how grateful they were that I brought this up, and we were all surprised how much we all had to say. I feel closer to them now more than ever. We didn't want to hurt our parents, so we kept them out of the conversation. There are things I'd really like to ask them, but I'm not ready, probably because I don't know if they are ready to answer!

Melinda: As a family, we took on a research project. We looked up all the ethnicities and cultures in our family tree. I have English, French, Scandinavian, and a touch of Miami Indian blood in me, so we did those, plus Korean, and the Western European mix that runs through Brian's parents. We looked at society, language, culture, the arts, current lifestyle—you name it. The kids were fascinated about some of our family holiday traditions that could be traced to centuries-old practices. Even my parents hadn't known where some of those traditions had come from. No one ever thought to ask; we just followed them. Then Brian and I did Culturegrams focusing on outward appearances. That stirred up a lot, too. Brian and I figured out that some of what we were dealing with really *was* culture clash.

Brian: The family research brought up questions about nature versus nurture. Growing up, one of the hardest things was the way Cheryl and I were different from our parents and Vicky. They just fit, you know? But Cheryl and I—sometimes one of us would react in ways that were considered pretty off the wall. Sometimes we'd both see things the same way and it would be us against Mom, Dad, and Vicky. After having read about Korean history, culture, and society, I wonder how much of those differences are actually hardwired into us.

In any case, getting things out in the open helped a lot. It helped me put a finger on things I'd experienced and felt over the years but had never fully understood. I got really sad, too, about having been adopted. I hadn't come face to face with that, maybe out of loyalty to the parents who raised me, maybe because I just wanted my family to be my family. I didn't want to think about having been given away. As a kid that would have hurt too much. Even as an adult it hurts.

I'm putting things into better perspective now, not running away from it with a joke the way I used to. Sometimes I think about looking for my birth parents. It would be nice to know about medical history and things like that, but I guess I'm a little afraid of what I might find. At this point I can honestly say I am grateful to my kids for the questions they asked. I hope I'm a better help to them now that I've helped myself.

Things to Consider:

- Do either you or your partner experience disparity between your ethnic or cultural identity and your physical appearance? If so, how does it affect your sense of belonging?

- Are there questions you have about your personal histories that remain unasked or unanswered? Do you have any ideas about what could help fill in the blanks? (For example, researching your cultural heritages like Brian and Melinda did.)

- Brian and Melinda's Culturegrams are in the resource section.

AFRICAN AMERICAN
LIKE ME?

Kori and Malaika

Kori: Africa was unlike anything or anyplace I'd ever experienced. As soon as I got off the plane, I felt like I'd come home. It was something deeply spiritual, and I don't think I was completely prepared for it.

Even though I felt at peace there, I was also quite aware of being an outsider. I have African heritage, but I'm from Michigan. In Africa I felt and was identified as American first, whereas in the States my identity had always been African American. My time in Uganda working for a nongovernmental organization was different from any other experience I'd ever had being black.

Working alongside people from many different countries, but mainly with Africans, gave me a different experience of myself. I came face to face with attitudes and opinions I'd grown up with that weren't necessarily true or valid.

Malaika was important to my life in Uganda from the beginning. She had a grace and courage that were at once inspiring and a little intimidating. At first I didn't know who or how to be around her, so I avoided her except for work-related things. I think she thought I was pretty full of myself, so it took a while for us to be comfortable with each other. Then we spent a couple weeks together as members of a team on a field assignment. The four of us had to rely on each other a lot, and we became friends. That's when Malaika and I really got to know and appreciate each other.

Malaika: Our time together in Africa was magical. Our work with the medical program was very intense yet satisfying. Health care in Africa is not what it is in the United States. We saw many things that most people in America do not see or want to see. Kori handled it well, and I was impressed.

Kori and I are both slow to trust. We both prefer having a few close friends rather than many friendly acquaintances. In my culture, there is a clear difference. As we became more comfortable with each other, I helped Kori with the subtleties of African culture. He already knew a lot about the history and politics involved, but actually living in Africa is different.

Romance in the midst of suffering is a strange thing, so our romantic involvement developed slowly. The lightness and joy of our relationship helped balance the seriousness of our work. When Kori proposed marriage, I knew I wanted to be with him forever. That was a simple decision. But where would we live? That was not so simple, and we discussed it at great length. I come from a large family, and we are very close. My grandparents left Belgium for Rwanda as medical missionaries, and my parents raised their family in Uganda. We learned to depend on each other through good times and bad. Many people in the United States don't understand who I am. I am African, even though my face is white.

Ultimately, it was Kori's professional opportunities in the United States that decided the matter for us. Also, after my experiences working with Americans, as a woman I felt I would have more opportunities in the States. I could continue my education, and there was always the option of returning to Africa.

Who Is This Man?

Malaika: When I first came to the United States, I thought I knew my husband. I was wrong. Seeing him with his old friends was like meeting a stranger. They used slang I'd never heard before. When we were with his friends and family, Kori even stood and sat and moved differently than when we were in private. In public among strangers, Kori's mannerisms were different again. In Uganda Kori had seemed confident. He hadn't minded not knowing something, or asking for help. Back in his hometown of Detroit, it was quite different. He was guarded and he approached problems with a wariness I didn't recognize. I wondered, who was this man I had married?

Soon after we arrived, Kori's family held a barbecue in our honor. It was an overwhelming afternoon for me. I overheard Kori's sister say, "There's another good black man choosing a white woman." His cousin responded, "Yeah, and she calls herself an African." I understand that I was a stranger to them at the time, but it still hurt deeply.

That night I asked Kori what was happening. He took me aside and did his best to answer my questions. He also explained the attitudes some African American women have about interracial marriage.

Kori: Introducing my wife to my family and friends was harder than I thought. It was one thing calling my parents to say I was getting married; it was another to actually bring Malaika home.

Even though I'd told them she was white, I wasn't ready for their prejudice. My friends were cool with it, but the cultural divide was wide with them, too. Other than asking if she had any sisters back home, they didn't have a lot to say to her. I felt at a loss, too, after being gone for two years. See, most of my friends haven't seen much of the world. It makes a difference, all right. We ran out of things to talk about.

I decided to widen my job search in hope of a fresh start. We ended up on the West Coast. It's less complicated, but I miss my family. Now Malaika and I have that in common, too.

The Counselors' Perspective

There are two things going on here. One is codeswitching, and the other is cultural identity. In minority communities, cultural identity can be hard won and closely guarded. Ethnocentrism can be strong when people have limited exposure outside their communities. There can also be a fear of outside influences. This was a factor with Kori's family and friends.

When cultures collide, you can run but you can't hide. Sometimes situations or reactions from other people reveal a difference or conflict that a couple might not even suspect is lurking. A couple create their own culture when in their own bubble. We each develop our own persona and role within relationships. These roles may not fit in the outside world where we have to adapt to different types of relationships and situations. This adaptation is codeswitching.

Kori is an accomplished codeswitcher. When he moved to Africa, he added another culture to his menu of codeswitching. Malaika, on the other hand, didn't realize Kori had other ways of relating.

When Malaika saw Kori camouflage into his environment, she didn't understand and became scared.

All of us codeswitch. When it happens among our inner circle, it can throw us for a loop. This is what happened with Kori when he returned home with Malaika. He codeswitched, trying to recapture the relationships he had with his friends and family. However, his family and friends experienced him differently and reacted accordingly. They felt left behind; in turn, Kori felt betrayed.

Based on her appearance, people identified Malaika as being white and expected her to fit the mold of the majority culture. Malaika was a foreigner in the United States, even though she didn't look like one. She felt angry at being denied her African identity. She was exhausted by the effort of explaining and wanting to be accepted for who she was.

What Has Helped

Kori: We never really talked about it before we moved to the United States, but I think we both figured that America is pretty liberal, so our togetherness wouldn't be a big deal. We were wrong. I went to college on the West Coast, which *is* pretty liberal. Going home with Malaika was another matter altogether. People's attitudes about my marrying a white woman hit me hard.

Thinking back, I took it for granted that my family and friends would automatically accept the woman I love. I thought they'd have the same outlook as me. This showed me that I'd grown away from my roots. I hadn't realized the extent of it. Malaika was looking to me to help her adjust, but I was in culture shock, too. I was feeling helpless on two fronts and didn't even realize it.

Malaika: It was very frightening for me to see Kori change before my eyes. I thought I had made the biggest mistake of my life trusting and marrying a man who was obviously not who I thought he was.

We were still in Michigan when I returned to Uganda for my father's sixtieth birthday celebration. Kori could not come, so I went alone. Being in the bosom of my family showed me how much I missed every element of home. In addition to the people I love, the sights and smells and tastes and ways of my country were comforts to me. I was reluctant to return and extended my stay by one week.

Back in Michigan my mother-in-law recognized what was happening. She sat us down and said we needed to find our way back to each other. Kori had thought that moving to the West Coast would improve our lives, but it wasn't until we dug into what was really bothering us that things began to turn around.

Kori: If she was going to be happy, Malaika needed to figure out who she was in this country. I realized I needed to be there for her in ways I never had to be for anyone else. I had to teach her to codeswitch. We talked about being African versus African American. I taught her slang. It felt good to return the favor; after all, she helped me with French and Swahili when we traveled in Africa.

I also talked with my family and friends. I educated them about Malaika and African culture. They asked questions they admitted to wanting to ask when they first met her, but were afraid to because they didn't want to offend.

Malaika: In Michigan I felt misunderstood. I had felt like an outsider among the African American community in Kori's hometown. I don't know why I assumed I'd fit in.

Kori: It was strange. People would see Malaika and label her white, disrespecting her sense of self. She tried explaining she's African, but they wouldn't accept it because of her skin color. On one of our worst days, she told me she felt like an animal on display at a zoo. She made the point that my family had been in the United States for over 150 years, and two years working in Africa hardly qualified me to be *African* American.

At first I was insulted, but after I thought about it, it made more sense. Here were people treating her badly for being a white African while they took pride in being African American. It was irritating.

Malaika: We're doing much better now. We can admit to not knowing something, and we're more open to learning from each other.

Kori: Now when we go to Detroit, Malaika is more confident. After all she and I have been through, I'm clearer about who I am, too. Now I refer to myself as a black American and my wife as an African. In our eyes, our future children will be true African Americans. And when the time comes, it'll be up to them to define what that means for them.

Things to Consider:

- Prevention is key. Discuss your understanding of your roles and how you adjust in different settings with different people.

- Talk about ethnocentrism in your families. For more on this subject, see the chapter titled Ethnocentrism.

WILL SOCIAL CLASS DIFFERENCES RUIN OUR RELATIONSHIP?

Hari and Lalitha

Lalitha: When I was growing up, opportunities were changing for girls in India, but not in my family. My father was a traditional southern Indian Brahmin. My mother was a proper wife who never challenged him overtly. I envied the freedom of girls from more liberal families; meanwhile, I complied to play the role of the dutiful daughter. From my parents' point of view, my opportunity to study made them proud; however, they expected I would return to India to marry well, just as my older brother had done. They didn't know I was focused on escape.

Hari: I was attracted to Lalitha's bright spirit right away. She was so unlike the other serious Indian women I knew. Lalitha was fun loving and had a great sense of humor. We biked everywhere and went to concerts. She wanted to try skiing her first winter in Indiana and she'd never even seen snow. She seemed committed to leading her own life separate from her family's upper-class lifestyle, where someone like me is beyond unsuitable.

It's not as if my family are untouchables. We are proud middle-class Punjabis, owners of a successful family business. But In India, my world is very different from Lalitha's. My childhood memories are of my parents as well as an aunt, uncle, two siblings, and three cousins working in the business twenty-four/seven. As the youngest child, my parents indulged my creative side. Though I knew the story of how my family migrated west when the British partitioned part of India into Pakistan, my childhood was safe and stable, more so than that of my older siblings. It seemed natural for me to love adventure and dream about studying abroad. I was very eager to study in the United States.

Lalitha: Hari and I were part of a small Indian student community without worries of social class, religion, or regional differences. Hari introduced me to things I had only imagined in India. It was intoxicating. We studied, lived in the moment, and had a fabulous time. We decided to get married when I finished my undergraduate degree. Even though I was rebelling against my family traditions at that time, for reasons I can't explain, I was set on being married at home. I wanted my wedding in the Hindu tradition. Hari was skeptical, but agreed.

Our Wedding Was an Emotional Monsoon

Lalitha: Though my father was disappointed in my marrying below our class, he was soothed because my siblings made him proud. My brother had returned from the United States, got a fabulous job, and married exactly whom he was supposed to. My younger sister was engaged to the son of my father's close friend. Also comforting to my parents was the fact that Hari's family lived thousands of miles away in northern India, and that distance would save both families the stress of celebrating holidays together after the wedding.

Our wedding ceremony was as beautiful as I had hoped, but the reception held numerous slights against Hari's family. On the surface, my family were perfect hosts, but in subtle ways, everything from the seating at the dinner to quiet remarks about Hari's family's clothes and regional dialect were pricks to cause discomfort. I know family friends sitting near Hari's family asked intrusive questions just to accentuate the social class differences. It was cruel. I had lived in the United States long enough to have changed my feelings about Indian classism, so I was deeply hurt that my family couldn't overlook class and regional traditions on my special day. We went back to Indiana right after the wedding, and my relationship with my parents felt stiff for a long time.

Hari: I wasn't surprised about how Lalitha's family treated my family at our wedding. It was the same old Brahmin classist stuff. I didn't like it, but I decided not to react to it because we were going right back to the United States. I didn't want to spoil anything for Lalitha. Secretly I was resentful and I never talked about it. I realize now I was naïve when I thought I could put the insults behind me as if they had never happened.

Distance Makes Denial Easier

Hari: Our first years of marriage were an extended honeymoon. After graduation, I got a corporate job while Lalitha finished her master's degree. We worked hard, played hard, and socialized with our Indian expatriate group. They were like a warm, validating family.

Four years ago, Lalitha was offered a good job in Seattle. When we arrived, I was surprised my professional opportunities were so limited. All I could find was inconsistent contract work. The upside to the poor job market was I had time to dive into my creative work. Two years ago a friend and I started a graphic design business. Financially we are still in the start-up mode, but professionally, I have never been happier.

Lalitha: I pushed for the move to Seattle because I thought the corporate world would be exciting. What I found were grueling deadlines and pressure. Looking back I don't know what I was thinking. When Hari and I first married we talked about our dream of a balanced work and family life with children at the center.

I never wanted to be an older mom. For several years now I have watched all my Indian friends and my younger sister get pregnant and stay home to raise their children. Now that I am pregnant I realize I have deep feelings about the way I was raised with a loving mother at home. I am shocked to find I have the desire for the kind of Indian family life I was raised with, including some of the privileges. I want to move from our one-bedroom condominium to a proper home with a yard. I want Hari to make enough money so I can stay home when our baby is born. I want my parents to come to visit and help for a couple of months after the baby arrives, because that is our tradition, the welcoming of new life and living as extended family.

Hari: We are having a hard time since Lalitha got pregnant. Suddenly she's become super Indian. We have started to argue in a way we never have before.

Through my career change I discovered I am more laid back about material things. I love Lalitha, but I want our relationship to be egalitarian. Lalitha never acted like a privileged princess until she got pregnant. What is happening to my modern wife? I believe she can work *and* raise our baby, just like my aunts and mother did. If I work like a maniac to make up the financial difference just so Lalitha gets to have the lifestyle of a privileged stay-at-home mom, what does that say about me? Am I just the meal ticket?

The Counselors' Perspective

Hari and Lalitha have relationship strength in their shared collectivist culture country of origin. Additionally, they have been successful in the way they have worked to blend their Indian cultures in the early years of their relationship. Now, with Lalitha pregnant, their social class world view experiences are becoming a powerful issue to negotiate. Social class and regional or ethnic expectations resurface every time a couple goes through a life transition. Hari and Lalitha have evolved from the stage of developing intimate relationships and career development to life as a couple with children.

Circumstances have protected Hari and Lalitha from meaningful discussions about roles and social class until now. As expatriate university students, they initially bonded around the opportunities for adventure and freedom of expression they found in the United States, an individualist culture. As a young adult, Hari was moving toward personal and professional opportunities dependent on ability, not family background. Lalitha was moving toward the autonomy women have in a large, individualistic country.

Additionally, in Indiana, Hari and Lalitha had the small Indian student community that, because of its size and young adult population, gave them positive Indian identity and cultural refueling without the judgments of social class or regional differences. It was an idealistic, supportive bubble. When Hari and Lalitha left Indiana, they left their tolerant expatriate Indian "family" and did not find a way to replace it in Seattle. In the transition from couple to family, they will need to find some support for cultural refueling.

They both knew they wanted children but had never talked about the expectations they had of each other when the time came to transition from being a couple to a family. In six years of marriage, Hari and Lalitha avoided talking about the meaning of social class, roles, and the privilege provided by wealth because of the painful experiences at their wedding in India.

In the United States, we talk openly about socioeconomic status, money, and economics, yet we shy away from judgments around social class differences. We don't talk about psychological loyalty to social class that may lie dormant until well into a couple's relationship. The best way a couple can deal with social class differences is to deconstruct them. For most people, it helps to externalize the social class discussion and talk about social class as culturally experienced roles and expectations without judging them. It helps to understand that social class is part of your identity. Many people carry the stories of social class slights for years without realizing how poisonous that can be to the relationship. When a couple has social class differences, the goal is to understand how it operates in their relationship. Then they can talk more honestly about class prejudices and social class misunderstanding without being defensive. Eventually, as a couple, they find their own compromises, their own middle ground.

What Has Helped

Hari: At first I was so shocked at what I considered a flip-flop in Lalitha's attitude about social class, roles, and her parents' wealth that I didn't think much about my part in the problem. After the wedding we flew back to the United States and never discussed the gaping space between our families' lifestyles. The prejudice I felt from her parents and the insult to my family at the wedding were all I could think about when Lalitha started to talk about having her parents living with us for a couple of months after the baby arrives. I got pretty emotional. I felt like they would be constantly judging my middle-class background and sizing me up as less valuable a person. I'm a naturalized United States citizen now, so I'm not putting up with that kind of prejudice ever again.

Also, it was easier to blame Lalitha's family and their attitude than be honest with myself that my parents had resentments, too. They are proud of their middle-class status and were upset I married a Brahmin. When I told them Lalitha was pregnant, they expressed concerns the social class difference would make it difficult for us to visit India as a family. They have a point. Except for a few holidays, Lalitha and I have visited our families separately since the wedding. When we become three, it won't be possible to keep everything so separate. Extended family and traditions are important to us both. We agree we want our children to love both sides and not be caught in the middle. I am trying to let go of being uptight when Lalitha's parents' extravagant gifts arrive. I don't have to react to it as an insult. It's their tradition to give.

When I feel threatened by her family's influence, it has been easier to call Lalitha a Brahmin snob than to face the fear that as a father, I really do feel an obligation to raise my income and provide for my child. My company is young and Lalitha has been supportive so far. But can I be the kind of provider I know I want to be? There are many unanswered questions; fortunately, Lalitha is starting to realize she will have to compromise about working to get some of what she wants financially. In America, I can't pay for it all.

Lalitha: I have been pining for traditions from home but have mostly kept quiet because our regional differences are all mixed up in Brahmin-Punjabi differences, which are hard to talk about. I am starting with small steps, such as letting Hari know when I want to dress Indian if we are going out, and letting him know this is of my cultural heart, not a rebuff at his sisters, who can't afford silk fabrics. I want Hari to know some of the things my parents want to do for the baby are my traditions. We don't have to consider their wealth a slap in the face just because we will never live like they do.

We lost our Indian American "family" when we left Indiana. In Seattle we landed in a neighborhood where there aren't many Indians. At the time it seemed OK to integrate into mainstream culture, and we have been surrounded by it ever since. Even Hari's business partner is of Irish heritage.

When I talk to American friends about my family or show pictures from home, I can tell many of them are put off by my family's wealth. It is not politically correct to miss so many things from my life in India, and I feel so disconnected not being able to talk about it. It is strange to feel ashamed about things I thought were normal.

In my student days I was proud to rebel against my family's expectations, but with a baby coming I am more concerned about financial security. I miss having my family nearby. In Seattle, I have felt it necessary to hide a big part of myself to fit in and make my American friends comfortable. Now I see how hiding who I am has made me lonely and could make me depressed. I have to figure out who I am as an Indian American. Hari and I want to be good parents, so there's a lot to figure out.

To balance our inside and outside worlds, Hari and I have been calling our relationship a "mixed marriage." It gives us some peace to make a big deal of differences that don't show, even if our American friends don't really understand. We've also realized that we have to take a chance and make new Indian American friends. We need some of the cultural comfort we had in Indiana.

Hari: Lalitha and I want our baby to be proud of his Indian heritage, not afraid to talk about it because of regional family conflicts. We will keep talking to our parents about our hopes and dreams for our life in Seattle, while working on accepting them for who they are. It's a relief to admit there are rich traditions from both sides of the family. I miss some of my traditions, too. Lalitha's parents are coming for the birth of the baby. When they leave we are bringing my parents over for a couple of months. All of them will spoil the baby in their own ways while they visit. We don't have to be so uptight. Ultimately, we are the ones who will most influence our child. We're talking realistically about balancing work and a family so Lalitha can be home as much as possible. We're off to a start on the changes we need to make, and that's good enough for now.

Things to Consider:

The following are questions about social class and social class attitudes that you and your partner should discuss. If you get stuck or the conversation gets uncomfortable, write some of your answers down, put them away for a week, and try again. If it is still hard to talk about, consider getting some professional coaching on the subject of social class and role expectations.

- How do you define social class? Before discussing it with your partner, take a moment to think about it or make a few notes on how you define your social class and the messages you got as a child.

- How did your family's social class affect your world view growing up? How about now?

WHAT'S THE REAL PROBLEM?

Nora and Quinn

Nora: I'd love to be able to say that we met on a moonlit night in Paris. The reality is we met over the Internet. Not quite as romantic, but it worked for us.

Quinn: At first I was reluctant to use Internet dating, but I'd tried everything else I knew how to do and wasn't meeting women I liked. When I put up a profile I was surprised how many women from all over the country responded. It was flattering and scary. You hear a lot about weirdoes on the Internet.

Nora's profile piqued my interest. Something about how she described herself and her values struck a chord, and I decided to take a chance. After some casual e-mails, we started corresponding regularly. Her sense of humor helped me relax, and after a while she became someone I felt I could open up to, regardless of the distance. By the time we met in person, we'd known each other for almost eighteen months.

Nora: Quinn wasn't the only one wary of weirdoes online. It had been a while since my boyfriend of three years and I broke up. I was ready to meet someone again, but wanted to take it slow because I didn't want to repeat old mistakes.

To be honest, I dismissed Quinn's profile at first. There were too many red flags: he was older, had kids, and lived half a country away. Then I got his charming e-mail and just had to answer.

Since Quinn was on the East Coast and I'm from the Southwest, we decided to meet in the middle. We both love the outdoors, so Colorado seemed like the perfect place. If it turned out we didn't mesh, we could go our separate ways and still be someplace we'd both enjoy on our own.

My parents were totally against it. They were appalled at the idea of me going off to meet a strange man. How many times did I hear, "Are you crazy? He could be an ax murderer!" The fact that we'd been e-mailing, then talking and Skyping for months didn't mean much to them. My parents are pretty old fashioned.

Anyway, I trusted my gut and am glad I did. Quinn and I clicked. We felt as if we'd known each other forever. We decided to marry a year later, which meant one of us would have to move. Quinn runs his family's business and my job situation wasn't ideal, so I volunteered.

Quinn: We got married in Nora's hometown. Our honeymoon was a cross-country drive, taking all her worldly possessions in a U-Haul truck out to New Hampshire. We took our time and it was great. It was during that trip that we began to realize just how different our backgrounds were. We'd talked about them before, of course, but we'd paid more attention to what we had in common than the differences.

I come from the quintessential Yankee family. My family history here goes back to the early 1800s. New Hampshire is in my blood. I went away for college and have traveled a bit, but this is home for me.

Nora: My dad is African American, my mom's from Burma, and I grew up in New Mexico. It's an unusual combo. Needless to say, people can't really tell what I am. In the Southwest most people assume I'm a Latina because of my dark complexion.

New Hampshire was like a foreign country to me. It was like being in the Twilight Zone; everyone I passed in the street had the same reaction. Their bodies would continue down the sidewalk, but their heads would swivel around with their expressions saying, "Who are you? What are you doing here?"

I got depressed. It was hard to motivate myself, make decisions, or enjoy life. I figured it was because I was a stranger in a small town where everybody knows everybody and there aren't many people of color. It started taking a toll. Quinn and I were sniping at each other, and we started wondering if we'd made a mistake. The scariest part was when we both said this out loud.

Mergers

Quinn: My first wife, Marilyn, died shortly after the birth of our second child. It took me years to even think about dating again. My friends and family kept setting me up with eligible women, but nothing came of it. Besides, everyone in this town had known Marilyn. I had to cast a wider net.

Nora is wonderful. The thirteen-year age difference isn't that big a deal for us. I'm in good health and keep myself in good shape.

Nora: Marrying Quinn seemed so natural. I knew we belonged together, but once we settled down into real life, things changed. Quinn was happy and wanted me to be, but we were in *his* comfort zone. Moving to New Hampshire was a huge leap of faith. I'd never been that far from my family for so long. And I became an instant mother, too. Because Quinn's daughters had been so young when their mother died, we bonded fast. They started calling me "Mom" right away. I loved it, and at the same time, it scared me. I didn't know what to do. Being a parent is a huge responsibility.

I was reluctant to tell Quinn how lonely I was because I didn't want him to worry. He could tell something was wrong. But when he would ask, I'd say everything was fine until he finally quit asking. Talk about our cultures colliding! We were both raised with different versions of "Hear no evil, see no evil, and speak no evil." We decided to see a therapist to work on becoming a blended family. That was a smart thing to do; it helped a lot, and life within our four walls operated more smoothly.

Outside, though, things got more complicated. People can look at us and tell that the girls aren't mine by birth. For example, when I took the girls to their activities, people would ask if I was the nanny. When I brought it up, Quinn said the townspeople weren't being racist, just "comfortable." What's that supposed to mean?

Quinn: Nora got lots of looks in town because people were curious, not racist. But when we'd go where no one knew me or my family, I could see it was bad. Before, we thought our ethnic differences added spice to our relationship. We'd talked about them a lot, and appreciated how much our differences helped us grow as people. Now we saw them as complications. We felt that if we didn't get a better handle on them, we were in danger of losing each other. After a while, though, it felt like we were spinning our wheels. We kept having the same conversations (and arguments) over and over without getting anywhere. It was frustrating.

Nora: What's that definition of "crazy"? When you do the same thing repeatedly with the same result, but keep doing it hoping things will change? That was us.

The Counselors' Perspective

Problem solving is a process we go through many times each day without even thinking about it. However, in tough conflict situations, it's imperative to approach the process in a deliberate, mindful fashion. Here are basic problem solving steps:

1) Define the problem.
2) Brainstorm possible solutions.
3) Develop an action plan.
4) Implement the plan.
5) Assess the results.
6) If things change for the better, celebrate your success. If things aren't better, go back to the appropriate previous step.

It's hard to fix something that isn't clearly identified. Sometimes the hardest and most important part in problem solving is defining the problem. Solutions to a problem that's not the *real* problem won't get you very far. In Quinn and Nora's case, they thought the issue was obvious: their ethnic and cultural differences. They did all the right things to address this, but their solutions still didn't help. What was really going on?

Quinn and Nora had actually addressed their ethnic differences quite thoroughly. The conversation was open and the topic was safe to revisit at any time. What they had not considered were the finer, more nuanced points of their differences based on geography and developmental stage.

Let's start with geography. As with so many of us, it didn't even cross their minds that moving from one region to another could be a major cultural shift. Using the Culturegram exercise, Nora examined potential sources of her depression and realized that she was keeping up fine with her relationships in New Mexico. However, what she missed and could not replace were the particular sunshine and dry heat, the vast vistas, the flavors and smells of the Southwest and her parents' kitchen.

Nora missed the pace of life and attitude of the people of New Mexico. She was suffering from culture loss and cultural grieving without knowing what they were. Happy and excited to be with Quinn and the girls building their life together, she unconsciously believed that missing the life she had lived as a single woman would somehow be disloyal to her new family. By comparing their Culturegrams, both Quinn and Nora were able to see these losses and differences more clearly and objectively, and were able to address culture clash in new ways. In doing so, they also got to know each other on a deeper level.

Let's move on to developmental stage. This was Nora's first marriage and Quinn's second. Nora was hoping for and expecting all those first-marriage experiences new brides dream of: romance, cozy dinners alone, social gatherings with new friends. Once they got back to New Hampshire, Quinn picked up the threads of his existence and was quickly immersed in the demands of his daily routine. For him, the honeymoon truly was over. Work and parenting took up a lot of his time and energy. His life in New England was already fully formed, but Nora had left her life behind to enter Quinn's midstream. Everything was safe and familiar to Quinn. Everything was new and threatening to Nora. As a competent, intelligent woman, she expected herself to be able to adapt quickly and successfully. She was disappointed with herself when she felt ignorant and weak.

Not having her support network nearby was another issue. Her collectivist world view made being away from her friends and relatives especially hard. Due to distance, Quinn didn't get to know Nora's friends the way Nora got to know his. Quinn's circle tried to include her, but Nora didn't understand all the old jokes and references they shared.

The merging of two lives was unbalanced in Quinn's life's favor. Quinn didn't realize his bride would need so much of his help adjusting. In addition, her cultural background led her to say nothing about it. Instead, she held her feelings inside, started to doubt herself and her life with Quinn, and got depressed. Since so much of Quinn's time, attention, and energy were directed to elements of his "previous" life, Nora felt that Quinn was not totally committed to her.

Another issue facing them was that of forming an identity as a multiethnic, blended family. This is where Nora had life experience that Quinn and his daughters lacked. Seeing themselves as outsiders was not part of Quinn's family's world view; it was definitely part of Nora's. Nora took things personally and tried to deal with them alone. It changed when the focus became collective.

What Has Helped

Nora: When I got depressed, I started therapy where we focused on my sense of belonging. The therapist encouraged me to talk with my parents about their experiences as a multiethnic couple. I realized how deeply I had been affected as a kid by people's reactions to how we looked as a family. That kind of preprogrammed me to assume that this was the major issue facing me and Quinn. I also learned that after she left Burma, my mom experienced similar situations to mine, and that she dealt with them the same way, by holding everything in and hiding her feelings. So I guess I came by those strategies quite naturally.

Once I clarified that I was suffering from culture loss and needed to do my grieving, it felt like a huge weight had been lifted. That's how I knew this was the real problem, and it helped me explain it to Quinn. Quinn can be stubborn, but he eventually admitted that he'd totally missed the cues. So we worked on it *together*. I vowed to talk to him about what bothered me, even if it went against my nature. Quinn vowed to try to see things through my eyes. He was used to focusing on the practical side of life—running the business, taking care of the girls, checking in on his parents, everything he'd done before we got married. He realized that if we were going to survive, he needed to make our relationship a priority in ways that worked for both of us. There aren't enough hours in the day for him to do everything he'd been doing, so he had to find ways for other people to pick up some of the slack. That's something he still struggles with.

We found ways that I could help with this, and that has helped me find my place here. I'm getting to know people better and making friends. I also see how I kept myself at arm's length from my new life, because I was still grieving my old one. I had been afraid that I wouldn't do a good job, that I'd come up short. It's hard to step into an instant wife and mother role. Now I see that I was being unfair trying to compare myself to Marilyn. I'm doing my best to give that up and be myself. I was also constantly thinking that other people were judging me when they weren't. They were trying to get to know me in their way. Getting to know more about the local mind-set has helped a lot.

Quinn: There are two more things that stand out in my mind as making big differences. As a family, we talked about the racism

Nora and her parents faced and how it affected them. Living in a small white community, my girls and I had never been subject to prejudice before. Being part of a mixed ethnic family was new to us, and that's where Nora was able to help. We could also help her see the difference between racism and New England stoicism. New Englanders are not naturally warm, effusive people, and Nora took that personally.

Carving out newlywed time has also really helped. We're lucky in that we have plenty of people willing to take the girls for an evening or a weekend. Nora and I have been concentrating on us. I want her to know and feel, every moment of every day, how much I love her and how dedicated I am to her and our marriage. The stronger we are as a team, the better life is in all its facets.

I realized that Nora's done more adjusting to our new life than I have. Now I join in on some of Nora's Skype conversations, and some of her friends have visited, so I'm getting to know them better. We visit New Mexico as often as we can, too, because we all want to know and share her love of the things we can't substitute in New Hampshire. Between visits Nora's mother mails cooking ingredients so that Nora can have the foods and flavors she misses. And we're finding restaurants that have some of the things she gets cravings for. The girls love it, because it's opening up a whole new world for them. Nora is a wonderful role model for them, and I hope they follow in her footsteps to explore all life's possibilities when they are grown.

It's been a balancing act attending to all our needs as individuals, as a couple, as a family. I'm getting more used to the changes now and am feeling really good. I'm more relaxed than I have been in years, and Nora and I are closer than ever.

Things to Consider:

- Is what you are doing to solve a problem in your relationship not working? It could be that you need to retrace your steps in the problem solving process. Are there hidden perspectives that you may not even have considered?

- Where are you each developmentally? Is one of you entering another's life midstream? If so, what can be done to achieve a sense of balance?

WHY KEEP OUR RELATIONSHIP A SECRET?

Curtis and Mark

Mark: Curtis is the love of my life. We've been life partners for almost six years, and as far as I'm concerned, we're married.

Curtis: I feel the same way. We've had our ups and downs along the way—plenty of downs—but we powered through them all, so it's mostly ups now. We met through mutual friends when both of us were fairly new to this area. At first we just hung out together, exploring the city, trying restaurants, things like that.

Mark: There was a mutual attraction right from the start, but we didn't really address it. When we met I had just come out of a bad breakup, so I wasn't looking for a new relationship. Curtis was this cute guy who was fun to spend time with. That's all I wanted. Before long it turned into something else.

Curtis: I hadn't had many boyfriends before. I was still coming to terms with being a gay man and what it meant to me. What did it mean to me? It meant finally allowing myself to be the person I always fought to keep down and deny. Growing up, I didn't want to be gay. I wanted to be "normal." In other words, I wanted to be straight, and I'm not. Now I have a new definition of what "normal" is and can honestly say I'm a lot happier.

Denial Can Be a Powerful Thing

Mark: Six years ago things weren't as solid as they are now. We still had our own apartments, even though we spent all our time together. I kept telling Curtis it was a waste of money to have two places, but he was stubborn. Still is.

Curtis: Yeah, it took a good long while for me to admit that living with Mark was the right thing to do, the only way to be. You have to understand, it's not easy for a black man to come out. I left everything I knew, everyone I loved, including my son, back in Pennsylvania when I realized I couldn't live undercover anymore. I had a beautiful wife and son who I loved and who loved me. I had it all. My wife and I both had good jobs. We owned our own home in the suburbs and had the folks out for weekend barbecues. To the outside world, I was a black man who had *made it*. But I couldn't take it any longer. Talk about a cliché: I couldn't live the lie. So I got a divorce, and under the guise of getting a job across the country, I left. Being a gay man in the black community is not OK. I come from a proud family. I didn't want them, especially my son, to be burdened by my reality.

Mark: When we started getting really serious, Curtis's son, Jamal, was thirteen. It was a tough time. I wanted to be in a committed relationship, and Curtis hadn't even come out to his family. Curtis used to fly to Pennsylvania a couple times each year to spend time with Jamal. He didn't have to tell anyone about me. By the time Jamal started flying out here for vacations, Curtis and I had moved in together. Our place has three bedrooms and two bathrooms, so it's easy to look like we're just housemates. Curtis still doesn't want Jamal to know we're a couple. As far as Jamal knows, I'm his dad's best friend and we share a house because it saves both of us money, which is true. Curtis says he wants Jamal to grow up without the stigma of having a gay dad. He says he doesn't want Jamal to question his own sexuality based on his father's, and above all he doesn't want Jamal to be embarrassed.

Curtis: I was really insecure about who I was. Mark had come out years earlier. He understood what I was going through to a point, but after one of Jamal's visits he'd had enough. He said I had to choose—either be honest, come out to my family, and let everyone know we were together, or he'd leave, because now *he* was living a lie. I didn't feel he really knew what it was like to be in my shoes. Mark came from a conservative Midwestern town, but what he went through was different, even though he couldn't see it that way. We started fighting all the time. It got to the point that I didn't know if it was worth it. I didn't want to lose Mark, but he was asking for so much.

Mark: Yeah, I'd been through a lot. I grew up in a little town where everyone knows everyone, which means everyone knows everyone else's business and feels entitled to it. Growing up "different" was not fun. I covered it well, though; I played baseball and ran track. I was a good student, too. The one thing I didn't do with the other guys was spend weekends in the city trying to pick up girls. I think people suspected at the time, but no one said anything out of respect for my family. We've been on our land since the Oklahoma land rush of 1889. My great-grandfather helped found our town. I don't think people thought anyone from a family so Oklahoman could be gay. To them I was just Mark, and I appreciated that.

By the time I was a teenager, the postwar boom years were over and a lot of families moved to the city. Our high school closed, and we got bused to the high school in the next biggest town. Hiding who I was got harder as I got older. I tried dating. What a disaster! The kids at the new school didn't know or care about my family history, so I no longer had that protection. I got jumped on a regular basis. The guys I grew up with had their own stuff to deal with at that school. We watched each other's backs for a while, but then they decided a fag wasn't worth protecting, so I was on my own. Over time I got pretty depressed, even considered suicide. But I didn't want the assholes to win. What saved me was my parents and my high school counselor, who pushed me to succeed. I got a good scholarship to a college those fools could never even dream of attending. I got out of there and haven't looked back.

Curtis's reluctance to let his family know who he is gets to me. I went through a lot growing up, too, and in the end my family supported me. I want him to take the risk. Even though it might take some time, I have faith his family will adjust. Doesn't he want his family to know who he really is? I don't understand.

Curtis: There's so much Mark doesn't get about what I'm going through. Yeah, he had to deal with a lot growing up. But it's one thing to go through this as a kid, and another thing to do it when you *have* a kid. Full disclosure means I might lose my family, including my son. Homosexuality is something that's still not talked about openly in the black community. Mark got help from his high school counselor, and even his friends, to a point. Me? I'm a black man in the professional world. That's hard enough. I risk a lot if I come out.

The Counselors' Perspective

The lack of understanding between Mark and Curtis happened on many levels. It was based on their different minority experiences. Mark thought that he fully "got" Curtis. He didn't, and Curtis knew it. However, even when Curtis tried to explain this to Mark, Mark couldn't hear Curtis because he was trying to understand through the lens of his own experience, his own reality, his own ethnocentric thinking. In addition, Mark had minimized the trauma of his own coming out story in the era of the early AIDS crisis.

It was hard for Mark to understand the general air of fear and resentment toward homosexuality still present in the black community. As a white gay man, Mark is a member of a minority group. As a black gay man, Curtis is a double minority. Membership in each group presents its own risks. Mark took Curtis's educational and professional success for granted. He didn't truly grasp how much harder it was as a black man to achieve success.

Curtis realized that discrimination based on skin color is hard enough. He was able to handle that; however, he wasn't sure he could handle it compounded with discrimination based on his sexual orientation. The risks spanned both his personal and professional lives. As he said, Mark was asking him to risk it all.

Curtis also knew he didn't "get" Mark. He didn't relate to Mark's experiences and saw them as an almost-best-case scenario for a gay man communicating with his family. He insisted that Mark didn't have it that bad. What he didn't realize was that there was more to the story. Mark entered adulthood as the AIDS epidemic was wreaking havoc in the gay community. There was little understood about HIV/AIDS; the fear was great, and the ostracism of gay people severe. The differences in time, geography, and skin color all influenced each man's experiences, adding to the trauma.

What both eventually came to realize is that suffering, healing, understanding, and acceptance are not a contest.

What Has Helped

Curtis: My family thought that homosexuality was the white man's way of keeping the black man down. My grandmother used to say that black men caught homosexuality from whites. She thought that black men with no pride turned gay to be more like whites. When so many black men were dying of HIV/AIDS, she said it proved her point; it was a white man's cancer that they spread to us to eliminate our race. How could I tell my family I was gay? How could I explain my family's attitude to Mark? This was a no-win situation.

Mark: Watching Curtis go through this was torture for me, too. I started having flashbacks about high school. I started remembering things I hadn't thought about in years. I'd been a good liar about my family being supportive of my coming out. What I didn't say was that when I came out to my folks, my father broke my nose. It was also the last day he ever said a civil word to me. He couldn't wait for me to leave for college. That way he'd never have to lay eyes on me again, and he could tell everyone his son was off to some famous university to make it big. What he didn't realize was that everyone in town already knew I was gay. To them I was an aberration, so that meant the rest of them were in the clear. No one else could be gay—not their sons or husbands. They were safe. They pitied my parents behind their backs.

The AIDS scare didn't do anything to help things. My mother told me to stay at school over breaks. It's not as if I wanted to come back. She didn't think I'd be welcome anywhere in town. The rumor was that I wasn't really at school; I'd left because I was sick and dying and contagious.

So once I left, I never went back. I wasn't welcome. My mother and I stayed in touch over the years. I got word to her through my aunt, her sister. Since my father died, I see my mother once or twice a year.

Being honest with myself helped me see Curtis's point of view. I was pushing him for the wrong reasons. I think I hoped his family would react differently from mine, that if his experience was a good one it would help me heal from mine. I wanted for him what I never got. I also sometimes wonder if there isn't a part of me that thinks if he gets the same reaction I got, we could be even closer.

Curtis: It would also be proof that it wasn't just you and your family, and it wasn't your fault.

Mark: Yeah. It's hard to be so alone. We've learned that we don't have to be. Whatever Curtis decides is up to him. In the meantime we have our life together, and I'll do what I can to support him.

Curtis: I'm still debating what to do. I want to tell my family, but I'm scared. It'll be a shock, and I'll have to help them absorb it. I need to find ways that help them see I'm still me, and that it's better to see the *real* me. My parents raised me to be proud, maybe too proud, because that's why I cut myself off from the people I love for way too long. I've learned that I can still be a strong black man, a good father to my son, a good friend to his mother, a loyal son to my parents, *and* a loving partner to Mark.

Things to Consider:

- If you are a double minority, how has membership in each group affected you?

- Has your quest to be heard and understood made it hard for you to hear and understand your partner? If so, how? Use your Culturegrams as starting points for this conversation.

WHEN IS LOYALTY OVER THE TOP?

Tony and Natalia

Tony: Natalia and I worked in the same department, so we interacted frequently. Initially I wasn't drawn to her. She seemed so career focused and, unlike me, always managed to get what she wanted from our boss. Then one day I walked in on her as she sat holding her cell phone to her ear, talking in some other language, with tears running down her cheeks. She ended the call fast and tried to hide her emotions. I'm still not sure what made me do it, but I suggested we go for a coffee break. I found out that afternoon Natalia had a compelling family story that changed my assumptions.

Natalia: Tony caught me completely off guard that day. This guy I thought was a total lightweight turned out to be a deep, caring person.

My family left Russia when I was five years old. What I remember of Russia is pretty vague; some family holidays, but more warm feelings than actual events. My vivid memories began after we arrived in the United States. A big one is my first day of kindergarten. I didn't speak a word of English. The teacher was kind and the kids were mostly accepting. In a few months I was as fluent as the other kids in my class and making friends.

America was not an easy transition for my parents. In Russia Mama had been a scientist and a political activist. My parents say in those days Mama was the passionate idealist and Papa was the practical realist. After a political rally, Mama was arrested and spent the weekend in jail. Papa feared for her life, thought he would probably lose his job, and who knows what other kind of black mark against the family might keep us kids from getting good jobs when we were grown. Papa insisted we emigrate.

As immigrants, my parents went from being respected professionals to doing hourly labor. Eventually Papa got a job as a program manager at a local non-profit agency, but Mama, who had been so successful in Russia, never rose from her position as a seamstress at a department store. When Mama gets in a bad mood she blames her activism for causing our family's departure and subsequent loss of status. Personally, I am glad to live in America, which has been so good to me, but I'd never say a word about that out loud at home.

As a child I was fascinated by the displays at Mama's store, and I credit the career I developed as a buyer to the fashion designs I saw there. At thirty-two, I've got a great position at a national department store. I tell Mama she is the inspiration for my success, but she's too bitter about her own losses to be humored out of her dream for me to be an academic.

Tony: I come from a big Italian American family so I am always drawn to people who make time with their family a priority. Nonna, my mother's mother, came to America as a war bride in 1947 on a ship after marrying my grandfather, the Italian American GI she met in World War II. They had six children. My father's family came a generation earlier, from Naples through Ellis Island. On both sides, most of us are still within a day's drive of Chicago. That's how close we are.

My family embraced Natalia right off; she's got old-fashioned manners and a great sense of humor. The only hassle I got was from my brother and a few cousins, who tease me about marrying someone who makes more money than I do. I think it's cool that Natalia's a go-getter and is career focused. I don't like my current job and she's been my best listener and coach as I figure out what I want to do next.

Loving Family or Too Much Family?

Natalia: Tony and I are friends as well as lovers. We love European history and languages and share interest in our family heritages. We went to Italy on our honeymoon and stayed with his relatives in different villages. Now we are planning a trip to Russia for next summer. I've heard my parents' stories, but since we left when I was young, I want to get my own impression of my birth country. I want to know if I will feel more Russian when my feet hit the soil.

We like variety in our lifestyle. Tony and I are into Saturday night clubbing and dancing whenever we get the chance. Careerwise we are both creative and might even start our own business someday. And we complement each other. Tony is not your stereotypical hot-blooded Italian. He is actually quite levelheaded and even tempered; it takes a lot to ruffle him. I'm the more intense type with ideas galore, but I get wound up when I am stressed.

Our stress usually comes from my family's demands on my time. Tony's family understands we need some couple space, but my family, especially Mama, is possessive. I feel caught in the middle between Tony and my family and I don't know what to do about it.

Mama and I have always been close. It started when we arrived in America. As the youngest child and the only daughter, I would come home from school, listen to Mama's homesickness for Russia, and try to make her feel happier. No one else was around in the afternoons so I was the one who taught her English. For a long time I thought it was my fault she never became fluent. In the early years my father worked two jobs and my brothers did odd jobs for neighbors after school. Later, when family finances were better, Mama and I were already an established team. As I got older, I started spending more time with friends, and she started to cling even harder. I love her, but I wish she would move on. Her demands for my time seem to be getting worse. Lately, when I come home after spending time with Mama, I feel down in a way I can't shake. It's starting to affect my relationship with Tony.

Tony: I adore Natalia and I've wracked my brain for ideas to help her with her mama, but her mama's demands are starting to get to me. I think Natalia's mama is actually jealous of our relationship. She has this psychic knack of knowing just when we've planned a special evening or an overnight out of town and she calls with some little crisis. Natalia feels guilty about her mama's life, so she either goes over or spends an hour with her on the phone. By the time Natalia is done talking to her mama, her mood is ruined. I understand about loving your family, but this is too much. I don't know what to say or do, but something needs to change.

The Counselors' Perspective

Natalia and Tony both come from collectivist families. The shared value of family relationships is one of the things that drew them together. Nonetheless, one reason Natalia and Tony are getting into conflict is because their families are at different stages of the acculturation process. The other reason is Natalia's mother has severe culture loss and grief that she has not been able to resolve, and she uses Natalia as an emotional lifeline.

Tony's family have been in the United States three generations. They still have a strong Italian identity because the core of the family has stayed in an area that has reinforced the family's ethnic identity. At the same time, as a third-generation immigrant, Tony makes many individualistic choices for his future that his grandparents or parents would not have considered. After a year of marriage Tony is losing patience with Natalia's loyalty and feelings of responsibility for her mother's happiness. He wants more time for their relationship, and he wants Natalia to set some limits with her mother.

Natalia is what is called a .5-generation immigrant. That means she was born in her parents' homeland but immigrated before puberty. Those who are .5-generation immigrants have vaguer memories and less attachment to their country of origin than their parents or older siblings. Usually, .5 immigrants acculturate easily, identify with the new country, and speak their adopted country's language without an accent. Their easier time with acculturation can make .5ers feel guilty when other family members struggle with language and cultural adaptation. The burden can be especially heavy when parents immigrate because of political or economic duress and get stuck in waves of culture loss, as Natalia's mother has done.

It's important to note the tremendous variety in how individuals adapt to losing cultural touchstones. Each person's innate resilience and personality traits factor into each family member's acculturation success or lack of it. Some people just get stuck for a while, and some people get depressed and stay depressed instead of adapting. People like Natalia's mother who are stuck in culture loss often cling to their loyalty to their homeland language and culture and expect the same from their children. However, the cost to the children can be high, often bringing on unexpressed anger or depression.

Natalia has been leading a double life. She can't share her bicultural perspective with her mother because her mother holds tightly to everything Russian and feels betrayed that the rest of the family has become so American. Natalia has tried taking space from her mother by avoiding phone calls and visiting less frequently. Her mother has reacted to the change by creating crises and accusing Natalia of forgetting the sacrifices her parents made to give her a good life in America.

Tony is frustrated, but he understands Natalia's dilemma. It will help if he and Natalia talk about culture as separate from, but related to, her loyalty to close family relationships. Once identified for what it is, Tony and Natalia can problem solve her issue as an adult child of immigrants stuck in a childhood role because family loyalty has made it difficult to question family patterns.

Natalia has been trapped in a no-win experience, trying to create an adult life of her own while still being a dutiful daughter. If Natalia and Tony create more consistency in the time Natalia spends with her mother, her mother will feel more honored. She may initially resist a more structured relationship but will eventually feel less abandoned. Creating a structure both Natalia and her mother can count on can help reassure Natalia that she is being a good daughter while enabling her to let go of the illogical concept that she is the only one who can help her mother.

In family situations like Natalia's, it might also be a good idea to help her mother cope with her depression. It may help Mama to figure out, with support from the rest of the family and medical help if necessary, if the depression is due to unresolved grief or if a physical problem is exacerbating her condition. It is also important to remember to do so gently. People with immigrant parents need to be mindful of how they seek help for a loved one with depression or other mental health problems, because many first-generation immigrants think mental health counseling or medication is only for the insane.

What Has Helped

Tony: Natalia's family, especially her mother, is so demanding. My family wants to see us but they are content with phone calls, drop-in visits now and again, and a couple of dinners a month.

Once Natalia and I started talking more openly about her mother's loneliness, her pride and self-imposed isolation, I was able to be more empathetic. This has helped me focus on the things I enjoy about her family, although it's still clear we need a strategy for change. I love history; they have great stories about Russian culture and politics from the 1970s and '80s, and they can talk forever on the Russian classics.

I also consulted Nonna and some other older relatives. That helped me better understand the immigrant story and Natalia's parents. Nonna had always talked about the village she came from, but not much about what it was like to leave Italy and not see her family for twenty years. Nonna told me she was so homesick she thought she would die her first year in the United States. She told me love for my grandfather, their church with its other Italian Americans, and the birth of my eldest aunt soothed her in the early years. Nonna told me she also knew immigrants who were bitter about their life in America because it was not the golden opportunity they expected. Nonna helped me understand and support Natalia rather than being impatient with her mother.

Natalia: Tony was right about Mama being jealous. It took me a while to acknowledge the pattern of her moods and our social plans.

Religion is what brought it to a head. My parents didn't raise us with any spiritual practice. After Tony and I married, I started attending Mass with Tony, first out of curiosity, then because I enjoy the liturgy and homily immensely. I don't know if I will convert, but we have agreed to raise our children in the Catholic church. When Mama found out, she was furious, saying if I go to any church it should be the Russian Orthodox church. Then she volunteered to start attending services with me.

One change Tony and I have made is the way we talk about what we can do that will honor my family loyalty and still give us the freedom we need as a couple. The first decision was to stop telling Mama every little thing going on in my life. It is amazing what just that little change makes. We still talk every day, but more about work and gossip that is not focused on me. And now I change the subject or get off the phone, saying I'll call her later, when she gets critical or bitter. I am also calling at a more regular time every day and calling it "our time" rather than avoiding her until she is furious. And I'm being less available for calls and visits just anytime. To honor Mama, I've been asking more about her family history, learning more about Russian cooking and stories I can pass on to my children. I am trying to reassure Mama I won't forget my roots even though I consider myself an American.

Tony had to push me, but I finally talked to my father and brothers about stepping up to spend more time with Mama. I was surprised to find out they didn't know the extent to which she was leaning on me. They knew she could get blue about Russia and the career she lost, but my father and brothers didn't realize it was still as bad as it is. My father was the first one to say he was sorry Mama and I had kept so much from him. He's going to try some new ways of getting out with her and finding more Russian culture nearby. If that doesn't work, he is willing to get a referral for a counselor from his doctor. He thinks she might go if he goes with her.

My parents haven't been back to Russia since we left. First it was for political reasons, and then it was financial, because the three of us were going to university. Papa talked about going in recent years, but Mama seemed to lose interest in seeing the "new Russia." So, Tony and I invited my parents to accompany us on part of our trip to Russia next year. We've asked them to show us some of "their" Russia. They've accepted and that's made all of us really happy. My intuition says there are rough times ahead with Mama. I still have days when I relapse to feeling it's my job to make her happy, but Tony and I have some ideas that could help me stay centered on what we can do and what I have to let go of. And we'll all keep talking about it.

Things to Consider:

- Talk about your own family immigration or migration story and individual family members' adjustment. Keep in mind a regional migration can have an impact similar to that of moving between countries, depending on the age at which the move is made. Is anyone in your family stuck in the acculturation process? How is it putting stress on your relationship?

- Have a conversation about cultural refueling strategies— movies, food, literature, music, etc.—that might help ease the tension.

WHAT HAPPENS WHEN THE PAST COMES BACK TO BITE US?

Eve and William

Eve: William and I met at the soup kitchen where we both volunteer. It was his first time there and he was cutting vegetables while wearing a frilly, flowered apron. I had to laugh. It's an ugly, old-fashioned thing, reserved for newcomers to make sure everyone notices and says hello. But William, a man of great presence and confidence, wore it with aplomb. He made that silly old thing look dignified. Yes, he caught my eye.

William: When I met Eve, she was laughing at me. Her laugh was so infectious I couldn't help but laugh myself. She sat down next to me and introduced herself and we started talking like we'd known each other for years. We laughed and laughed. It was extraordinary. My wife had passed six years earlier, and I hadn't laughed much since then. My heart felt lighter than it had in a long time.

Eve: It only got better after that. Within just months, we were going to each other's family get-togethers. His kids and mine get along fine. I think they were initially worried about our relationship, but they feel pretty good about it now. We haven't married, we don't live together, and have no intention of either. I've been a widow for almost twenty years. My kids are thrilled I have someone in my life again.

William: Eve is glossing over some parts. Sure, we got along great and enjoyed each other's friends. But dealing with my extended family proved difficult. My family has large reunions every five years. We'll have anywhere from forty to fifty people, and they are week-long affairs. I come from a family of debaters. We'll talk politics, music, history, heck, we'll debate the latest Johnny Depp movie. After we'd been together for a couple years, another reunion came around and I invited Eve to join in. Everyone had already heard about her and could hardly wait to meet her. I thought Eve would fit right in. Meeting everyone at once was overwhelming for her, as you can imagine, but instead of feeling more comfortable over time, she felt less so and withdrew. I didn't understand.

When I asked her about it, she said she felt like an outsider, that people weren't giving her a chance. It hurt me that she wasn't giving my family a chance. I realized then that she generally keeps her own counsel with new acquaintances. Her friendliness isn't exactly an act, but she's very careful. I was surprised to learn she was so guarded.

Eve: It's true. I've always been an introvert. I thought perhaps meeting so many new people at once was part of why I felt like I was on the outside looking in. But those feelings didn't change over time around his family. It hurt when William accused me of overreacting.

William: I still say having the expectation that people won't accept you is an irrational emotional reaction.

Eve: But just because someone wants to accept you doesn't mean he or she actually does.

Historical Perspective

Eve: My grandparents came from Japan at the end of the nineteenth century. They farmed the land and, after saving enough money, ran a successful grocery store. This gave them influence and a position of leadership within the Japanese community. My grandparents took great pride in helping new immigrants get settled.

My father took over the store when he and my mother married. From the stories, life was good. Pearl Harbor changed all of that, of course. I was a toddler when we were sent to a relocation camp, and have no memory of leaving our home. My earliest memory is playing in front of our cabin with my sister. We accidentally knocked over a bucket of water and my mother scolded us for being wasteful. Clean, potable water was precious.

In hindsight I see that the camp years were horrible. I had no understanding of it then. It was just life as I knew it. Despite being treated unfairly, my father considered himself a patriot. He raised our American flag every morning, and we said the Pledge of Allegiance. If he had been younger and not had a family, I'm sure he would have enlisted. I believe he thought the truth would eventually come out, and things would be made right.

My mother, on the other hand, was not as forgiving. She was bitter at having to give up everything her family had worked to create. Even though it was never openly discussed, my siblings and I knew how she was feeling and absorbed it.

William: I'm Scotch-Irish and proud of it. When my people were kicked off their land in Ireland they went to Canada. As uninvited immigrants, my ancestors faced prejudice at every turn. They finally entered the United States, where they paid their dues. At least one member of my family has fought in every war from the Civil War to Vietnam.

When Eve and I compared notes, I felt that even though our families had come from opposite sides of the earth, we had immigration histories in common. But at the reunion it became clear that Eve had never overcome feeling like an outsider. I thought at our ages we should be beyond that. Family is the most important thing in my life. Eve's attitude toward my family made me weary. I didn't want to have to take sides.

The Counselors' Perspective

Before the reunion, Eve and William had a sound relationship. Time with the extended family kicked their issues loose. Legacies of hurt from long-buried, hurtful events still affected them individually and without their awareness. They both found themselves thinking and feeling things that, on the surface, didn't make sense. They each said or did things they later regretted, and didn't know why they couldn't stop themselves. When this happens, hidden trauma is often the cause. In Eve's case, her family's decades of experience with racism and prejudice, culminating in their internment during World War II, resulted in a heightened sensitivity.

Unresolved or hidden trauma is more common than most of us think and can wreak havoc in relationships. People become conditioned to watch for repeated threats, often without understanding why. It is an automatic self-defense strategy, an unconscious basic survival mechanism. Unless we learn something different and retrain ourselves, our amygdalae continue to scan and our bodies continue to react, even when the process is no longer necessary for survival. We can't turn it on and off like a light switch.

Identifying the behavior you want to stop or change is a beginning step. Then detective work comes in. Understanding where and how you learned to do it is a useful next step. As William discovered, this often involves uncovering family secrets. With new historical perspective and understanding, an unconscious, habitual response becomes an opportunity for deliberate decision making. Sometimes it's not possible to decipher the mystery or shed light on the origins of these behaviors. Nonetheless, it's necessary to be aware of automatic responses and develop other options.

Eve wanted to let her guard down. What hindered her was the unrecognized trauma. Just as Eve's family absorbed lessons about being Japanese, William's family absorbed lessons that resulted in ethnocentric thinking and behavior. Both families acted on these legacies, whether they realized it or not. Eve's well-trained amygdala had picked up on something important. With cooperation, both Eve and William were able to understand what happened at the reunion.

What Has Helped

Eve: It does not come naturally for me to speak about difficult emotions. I learned that this is an Asian trait; it's also a family trait. These feelings I had at the reunion shook me up, and I had to talk to my siblings to make sense of the situation.

Since my family has been in the United States for generations, I thought of myself as American. But when I investigated my family history more deeply, I realized we'd been raised with traditional Japanese values. Understanding this and looking at the tragedies my family experienced during and after World War II helped me understand why I always anticipated and expected prejudice and rejection. As newcomers and fledgling business owners, my grandparents couldn't afford to be caught up in conflict. They had to keep their heads down. I absorbed that, too.

By being sensitive to others' reactions to me I could protect myself and keep my feelings from being hurt. I never let myself fully belong. Looking back, I remember how I did that automatically at school. My Japanese American classmates and I knew without being told who we could talk to, play with, and be friends with.

After I understood why I was usually so cautious with new people, I was able to talk to William about it. I appreciated his family did their best to accept me, but still felt a distance that neither side could bridge. William would not accept this. Finally I asked him to take a leap of faith and, even if he couldn't understand it, to accept it as my truth. I asked him to take a truly objective view, and when he did, he had a sense of what I meant. That's when he decided to do some detective work of his own.

William: My father's younger brother, my godfather, for whom I am named, served in World War II and survived a Japanese prisoner-of-war camp. I was a child when Uncle Will went missing. We knew he'd been fighting in the Pacific, but no more than that. I remember the day he came home like it was yesterday. I didn't recognize him; he was so thin and frail. Everyone cried, even the men. We were all so relieved that Uncle Will had made it home, but he had a haunted look and wasn't the same. He never talked about what happened, and we kids knew not to ask.

After the war there was a hard and fast rule in our family: buy American. The unspoken rule was, don't buy Japanese-made products, even when all the best-quality electronic equipment was exported from there. I finally made the connection between this and Uncle Will's experiences in the war. Buying American was our family's way of supporting him, and it had turned into a way of life. Over time, we bought things made in Taiwan or Germany. But never Japan.

Eve always said that one on one, she was fine with everyone in my extended family. She only experienced the unwelcoming feeling when with the larger group. I think now maybe what she felt was the family's legacy of "don't buy Japanese."

Eve: I needed help to figure out how my childhood affected me. My siblings and cousins were able to tell me what my parents were like before the internment camp. I learned that my father was not always a defeated man and that my mother was once quite happy-go-lucky, not bitter and suspicious as I remember her. I realized that I grew up thinking that there was something wrong with me and all Japanese Americans. There had to be, otherwise why would we have been forced from our homes and sent away? Of course, I never asked questions or expressed these thoughts to anyone. That was not my family's way.

William: My family carried loyalty too far. We carried Uncle Will's pain for generations. I see that now and am sorry for everyone involved, especially my uncle. In a way, we colluded in prolonging his suffering by keeping it in the spotlight years after the fact. He never overcame his pain, and what we had for him was pity, not understanding. It makes me wonder what he and the rest of us would have been like if we'd done something different. Yes, Eve and I both had healing to do. That required forgiveness.

Eve: And courage and honesty. William was brave in talking to his family about what we felt was happening. At first there was denial; then there was debate. But afterward, people started researching family history and began telling stories. That was when I felt ready to join in. At the most recent reunion, we of the older generation stayed up late comparing notes about growing up. We laughed and cried, but mostly we laughed. When we were finally ready to go to bed, we noticed that many of the young people had stayed up to listen. We hadn't even noticed them, they were so quiet. They just drank up the stories all night long.

William: The kids were really surprised when they learned how the "buy American" tradition started. It was such a hard and fast rule, it was never even questioned. Once we talked it through we all saw how pointless it was. Now some of us even have Japanese cars! The most important result, though, was the fact that Eve was a full part of our family reunion.

Things to Consider:

- Can you trace any opinions, family rules, or expectations, whether spoken or unspoken, to traumatic events and experiences? If so, how do they affect you now?

- If mystery remains, what kind of detective work would help? Whom can you ask for information? What other resources are available to you?

- Compare notes. How do your family histories interface, especially when it comes to trauma and loss?

PART THREE

BRIEF DEFINITIONS

Below are some terms used in Mixed Blessings. *Please note these definitions reflect how we use these terms. Our intention here is to establish a common language with our readers.*

Culture: Culture is learned, not innate. Everyone is born into his or her native culture. Culture is all those things that we each have learned to value and enjoy in our community, including ideals, beliefs, skills, tools, customs, and institutions.

Cross-Cultural: Cross-cultural is more of an educational mode. Students, emigrants, diplomats, and those in international business learn about other cultures in order to understand them better (i.e., an employee would get cross-cultural training before going to live and work in Saudi Arabia).

Culture Shock: Culture shock sets in after the "honeymoon period" of migration or immigration. The differences between the new culture and the home culture bring on anxiety, homesickness, and sometimes depression. An example is getting depressed during your first winter in Minneapolis after having lived in Honolulu for twenty years.

Culture Loss: Culture loss appears initially as culture shock shortly after moving. It resurfaces time and again when life events in the new culture conflict with life expectations from the culture of origin. The older the immigrant is at relocation, the more severely culture loss may affect his or her mental health and family relationships.

Cultural Grieving: Cultural grieving begins with culture shock and the awareness of culture loss. Healthy grieving is necessary to develop a blended cultural identity. It resurfaces with transitions and life stage losses. Cultural refueling can significantly ameliorate pain and loss in cultural grieving.

Cultural Refueling: Cultural refueling is the process of returning physically or emotionally to the comfort of the home culture or culture of origin. Cultural refueling includes but is not limited to community, place, language, food, music, spiritual practice, and rites of passage. Access to cultural refueling is important for healthy identity integration, especially during life transitions that trigger cultural grieving.

Emigrate: To emigrate is to leave the country where you were born. Sometimes people emigrate by choice, perhaps to join family, and sometimes by necessity, perhaps due to economic or political problems.

Ethnic Group: An ethnic group is a group of people that share a common heritage consisting of a common language, a common culture that usually includes a shared religion, and common ancestral roots.

Ethnocentrism: Ethnocentrism is the tendency to believe that one's ethnic, regional, or cultural group is more important than any other. An ethnocentric person compares other groups to his or her own group or culture. Examples of this are considering your region's version of a particular culinary dish as the ultimate (Texas barbecue vs. North Carolina barbecue) or thinking your regional accent is the best one to have.

Expatriate: An expatriate is someone who lives outside his or her passport country. "Expatriate" is a term used for someone who lives away from their homeland for years. Expatriates are legal visitors. They do not become naturalized citizens of the country in which they are living. People usually become expatriates for work or diplomatic purposes or because they are spouses or children of those with work or diplomatic visas.

Immigrate: To immigrate is to relocate to a new country or region with the intention of remaining there and setting down roots. People who immigrate often become naturalized citizens of their adopted country. As in emigration, people immigrate for a variety of reasons.

Individualistic and Collectivist Cultures: On the individualist side are societies in which the ties between individuals are loose. Everyone is expected to look after himself or herself and his or her immediate family. On the collectivist side are societies in which people from birth onward are integrated into strong, cohesive in-groups, often extended families which continue protecting them in exchange for unquestioning loyalty.

Intercultural: Being intercultural means being able to move back and forth comfortably between two or more cultures. It requires collaboration by people from different cultures, ethnic groups, religions, etc., so that power is balanced.

Migrate: To migrate is to move from one region or country to another. As in emigration, people migrate because they have to or want to. Migration does not always connote a permanent move. Guest workers and people who are transferred by their employer to a new state are migrating.

Multicultural: Multicultural means moving beyond one culture. A multicultural person can relate to and participate in the cultures of more than one country, ethnic group, religion, etc.

Subculture: A subculture is an "in-group" within the majority culture. As in the definition above, the values and behaviors are learned, not innate. A difference is that we often, but not always, voluntarily join a subculture, such as the military or a college sorority.

Third Culture Kid/Global Nomad: TCKs or Global Nomads are living or have lived as expatriates with their parents. It is common for Global Nomads to have lived in two or more foreign countries and to speak several languages. They usually consider themselves multicultural and are comfortable in many environments. The downside is their many moves may leave them without a clear sense of cultural identity.

Balancing Your Life Priorities

How well your personal life is balanced affects your couple relation-ship. The purpose of this exercise is to give you a snapshot of your current level of satisfaction in eight life categories, listed below. On this scale, 1 is a low level of satisfaction and 10 is a high one. Decide on the number that best fits how satisfied you feel about each category and mark the spot. What messages did you get from your family culture about work-life balance? Discuss your results with your partner.

1	Career	10
1	Income	10
1	Health	10
1	Friends-Social Life	10
1	Marriage-Partner-Family	10
1	Personal Growth - Learning	10
1	Recreation	10
1	Spirituality	10

Personal Qualities

Personal qualities research in the field of intercultural studies has identified traits or acquired skills that can help individuals more easily navigate between cultural world views. In this exercise we use the term *world view* liberally to include regional and same-country ethnic subcultures as well as social class.

On a scale of 1 (low) to 5 (high), rate yourself on each of the following characteristics by writing a number beside each one and totaling them.

Dealing with Ambiguity: _____

How comfortable are you when you get mixed messages about what to do, how to be, or what to think?

Open Mindedness: _____

When you have an opinion and think you are correct, to what extent are you open to an opposing view?

Being Nonjudgmental: _____

How well are you able to refrain from judging others on the basis of your own personal standards?

Empathy: _____

How easy is it for you to understand another person's situation, feelings, and motives?

Extroversion: _____

How talkative are you by nature? Are you inclined to approach people for conversation, advice, or questions? For example, do you enjoy small talk at work or with a waiter in a restaurant?

Adaptability: _____
How easily are you able to change to fit new life circumstances?

Curiosity: _____
How strong is your desire to learn about and experience new things?

Sense of Humor: _____
Rate your sense of the ridiculous or enjoyment of silliness or irony.

Warmth in Relationships: _____
How easily do you express affection for people with whom you have close relationships?

Motivation: _____
How much do you consider yourself a self-starter who puts energy and action toward a goal or problem solution?

Self-Reliance: _____
To what extent do you depend on yourself to get things done and meet your own needs?

Strong Sense of Self: _____
How firm is your sense of values and individual identity?

Tolerance for Differences: _____
How would you gage your ability to tolerate cultural, spiritual, and social class differences at work, in your family, etc.?

Perceptiveness: _____
To what extent do you consider yourself someone who has keen insight or good intuition about people and situations?

Ability to Fail: _____

Rate your ability to pick yourself up and continue on after a mistake. This includes your ability to admit a mistake and learn from it with grace.

Total Score: _____

If you score less than 50, you have some work to do. If you're doing this with your partner, talk about ways to support each other in making some changes to increase your flexibility.

Notes:

Your Ethnic Heritage

When did your family immigrate? Dates and countries of origin:

Maternal:

Paternal:

If your family migrated regionally within the United States, what is that history?

Maternal:

Paternal:

What stories were shared over the years about your family's immigration and migration experiences?

How have your family's immigration and migration stories affected you?

Culturegram

The Culturegram builds on the exercise titled Your Ethnic Heritage found earlier in this resource section. It is a chance for you to do some thinking on family beliefs, values, and traditions. Through this, you can uncover patterns and legacies in order to develop insight about a "stuck" topic. The goal is to be curious, not judgmental, about what you discover. If you're doing this together, compare results and see what matches and what doesn't. By understanding where your views come from, it is possible to be more objective and prevent yourselves from taking things personally.

The Culturegram is a diagram that will look different for each person because we all have different experiences and histories. Even if we come from the same culture or ethnicity, subcultures exist and we are all uniquely influenced by our families.

You've met Tim and Valerie, and Brian and Melinda. Their Culturegrams provide models on the following pages.

Here are the instructions:

1. Agree on a general theme to focus your Culturegrams. For instance, Brian and Melinda focused theirs on their issue around physical appearances. Tim's and Valerie's were on their cultural values.

2. Draw a circle. Within the circle, write the answers to the following questions. The descriptions are for you to determine. Write as much or as little as you need to.
   a. Where are you from? (It's OK to put down more than one place.)

b. What cultural and/or ethnic heritage do you identify with?

3. Draw spokes. On each of these, write a belief or value about your theme that you picked up from the family you grew up in.

4. In a circle attached to the end of each spoke, write how the belief or value affects you now in daily life (e.g., I go with it; I reject it; etc.).

Compare and contrast your Culturegram with that of your partner.

- What do you have in common?
- What differences can you identify?
- How do all of the above affect you in your relationship?

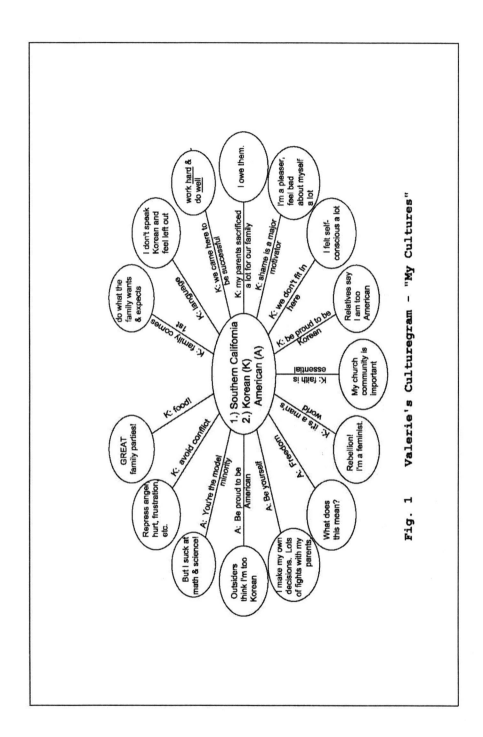

Fig. 1   Valerie's Culturegram - "My Cultures"

171

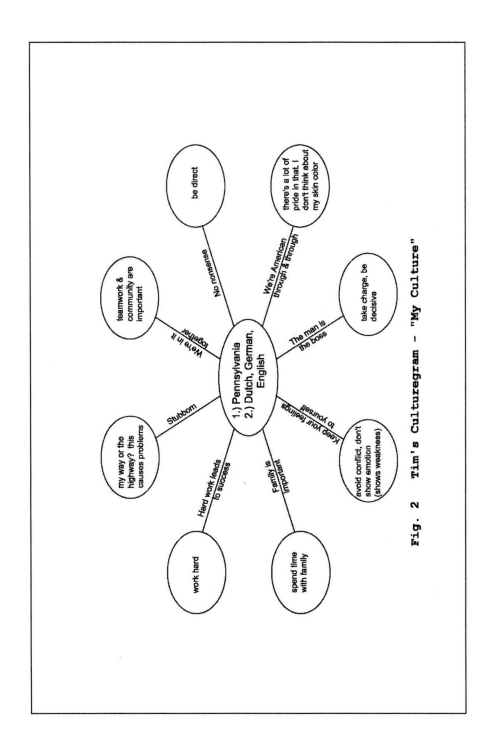

Fig. 2   Tim's Culturegram – "My Culture"

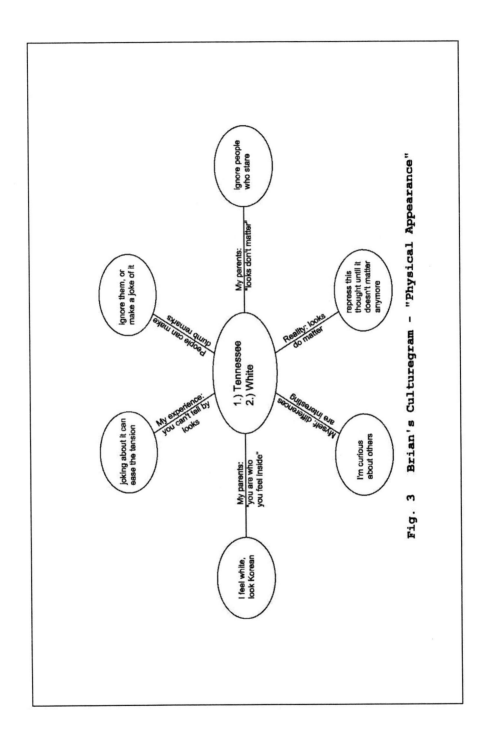

Fig. 3   Brian's Culturegram – "Physical Appearance"

175

.

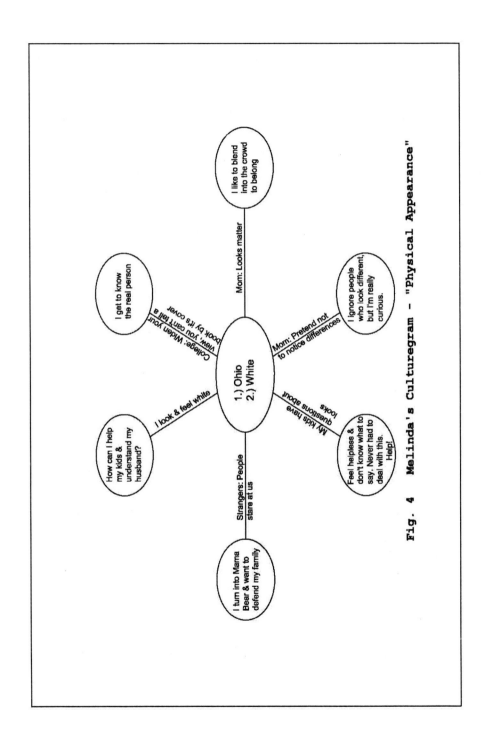

Fig. 4 Melinda's Culturegram – "Physical Appearance"

Cultural Conversation Starters

We have provided the following conversation starters as a way to ignite cultural curiosity about your own and your partner's family experience. First-generation immigrants have direct experience of family heritage, but the further someone is from the time of family immigration, the more is lost.

- Identify something about your family's cultural or ethnic history.

- How connected do you feel to it?

- Where did you grow up? What was it like growing up there?

- Did you and your family tell stories about people, places, and events from your home cultures? Were certain subjects avoided?

- Did one side of the family have more influence on you than the other? If so, how?

- From your perspective, why do you think that happened?

- What family traditions and rituals have carried over across the generations?

- How did you decide on which ones to continue?

- How did extended family influences change over time (for instance, after your marriage or with the birth of a child)?

- In what ways are you aware of having changed over time in the way you miss your home culture? More waves of homesickness or less? Are there certain times you can identify when you pine for home? What do you do about this?

- Has your family's home culture changed so that you fit less well when you visit relatives? What about when relatives visit you?

- How have *you* changed? Do you fit in less well when you visit relatives? What about when they visit you?

- How do your heritages connect and complement each other in your relationship?

- How do they clash with each other?

SUGGESTED READING

Here are some of our favorite fiction and nonfiction titles that address multicultural, multiethnic relationships.

Nonfiction

Childhood and Society, Erik Erikson, W. W. Norton & Co., 1963.

Beyond Culture, Edward T. Hall, Random House, Inc., 1989.

Culture From the Inside Out: Travel—and Meet Yourself, Alan Cornes, Nicholas Brealey Publishing, 2004.

A Different Mirror: A History of Multicultural America, Ronald Takaki, Little, Brown & Co., 2008.

Raising Global Nomads: Parenting Abroad in an On-Demand World, Robin Pascoe, Expatriate Press Limited, 2006.

Social Intelligence: The New Science of Human Relationships, Daniel Goleman, Random House, Inc., 2006.

Working Across Cultures, John Hooker, Stanford University Press, 2003.

The Geography of Thought: How Asians and Westerners Think Differently...and Why, Peter Nisbett, Simon & Schuster, 2010.

West of Kabul, East of New York: An Afghan American Story, Tamin Ansary, Picador, 2002.

Letters of Transit: Reflections on Exile, Identity, Language, and Loss, edited by Andre Aciman, published by New York City Library, 1999.

American Nations: A History of the Eleven Rival Regional Cultures of North America, Colin Woodard, Viking, 2011.

The Warmth of Other Suns: The Epic Story of America's Great Migration, Isabel Wilkerson, Random House, 2010.

The Genius of Language: Fifteen Writers Reflect on Their Mother Tongues, edited by Wendy Lesser, Random House, 2004.

The History of White People, Nell Irvin Painter, W. W. Norton, 2010.

Mixed: an Anthology of Short Fiction on the Multiracial Experience, edited by Chandra Prasad, W. W. Norton, 2006.

Unrooted Childhoods: Memoirs of Growing Up Global, Faith Eidse and Nina Sichel, editors, Intercultural Press, 2004.

The Global Soul, Pico Iyer, Random House, 2001.

Persepolis: The Story of Childhood, Marjane Satrapi, Pantheon Books, 2004.

Searching for Zion, Emily Raboteau, Atlantic Monthly Press, 2013.

Red Dust Road, Jackie Kay, Picador, 2010.

The Color of Water: A Black Man's Tribute to His White Mother, James McBride, Penguin, 2006.

The Spirit Catches You and You Fall Down, Anne Fadiman, Farrar, Straus, and Giroux, 1997.

Lost in Translation: A Life in a New Language, Eva Hoffman, Penguin Books, 1989.

The Long Way Home, David Laskin, HarperCollins, 2010.

Blindspot, Mahzarin R. Banaji, Anthony G. Greenwald, Delacourt Press, 2013.

Fiction

Cutting for Stone, Abraham Verghese, Random House, 2009.

Miracle at St. Anna, James McBride, Penguin, 2002.

The Elegance of the Hedgehog, Muriel Barbery, Europa Editions, 2008.

Hotel on the Corner of Bitter and Sweet, Jamie Ford, Random House, 2009.

Bel Canto, Ann Patchett, HarperCollins, 2001.

South of Broad, Pat Conroy, Doubleday, 2009.

The News from Paraguay, Lily Tuck, HarperCollins, 2004.

The House on Mango Street, Sandra Cisneros, Vintage Contemporaries, 1991.

The Namesake, Jhumpa Lahiri, Houghton Mifflin, 2003.

Native Speaker, Chang-rae Lee, Riverhead Books, 1995.

Ali and Nino: A Love Story, Kurban Said, The Overlook Press, 1996.

Gone With the Wind, Margaret Mitchell

Pride and Prejudice, Jane Austen

The Absolutely True Diary of a Part-Time Indian, Sherman Alexie, Little, Brown & Co., 2007.

Everything Is Illuminated, Jonathan Safran Foer, HarperCollins, 2002.

Where'd You Go, Bernadette, Maria Semple, Little, Brown, 2013.

Lost Hearts in Italy, Andrea Lee, Random House, 2006.

Fieldwork, Mischa Berlinski, Picador, 2007.

Bone Worship, Elizabeth Eslami, Penguin Books, 2010.

The Tricking of Freya, Christina Sunley, St. Martin's Press, 2009.